44 HORRIBLE DATES

DATES

EDDIE CAMPBELL

sourcebooks

This book is a memoir. It reflects the author's present recollections of his experiences
over a period of years. Some names and characteristics have been changed, some events
have been compressed, and some dialogue has been re-created.

Published by Sourcebooks, Inc.
P.O. Box 4410, Naperville, Illinois 60567–4410
(630) 961–3900
Fax: (630) 961–2168
www.sourcebooks.com

Library of Congress Cataloging-in-Publication Data

Campbell, Eddie
 44 horrible dates / Eddie Campbell.
   p. cm.
 1. Dating (Social customs)—Humor. I. Title. II. Title: Forty-four horrible dates.
 PN6231.D3C36 2012
 818'.602—dc23

2011051026

Printed and bound in the United States of America.
VP 10 9 8 7 6 5 4 3 2 1

This is a work of nonfiction. Unfortunately, and sometimes unbelievably, these stories of my horrible dates are all true.

9/27/2012

Joe,
I was told by a good "gay" source that this book is very funny. Horrible dates — we've all been there gay or straight!

Happy Birthday!
Love + Joy'
Jan

From the moment I picked up your book, until I laid it down, I was convulsed with laughter. Someday I intend on reading it.

—*Groucho Marx*

TaBLe OF COntents

The Dedication...............................ix

The First Date..................................1

A Word of Warning........................11

The Dates.......................................19

No Epiphany...............................227

Acknowledgments........................233

About the Author..........................235

▪◻ THE DEDICATION

For the 2 billion people in the world who are single, this book is dedicated to you. For the 50 percent of married people who will end up single, this book is dedicated to you.

I am dedicating this book to everyone who is single, was once single, and might forever be single. I am dedicating this book to anyone who has spent countless hours and countless amounts of money going on dates that were unforgettably terrible. I am dedicating this book to anyone who reads this and says, "My god, I have had it so easy." I am dedicating this book to every man and woman across our globe who has been on *one* horrible date, much less forty-four.

We all have a horrible date story or have at least

heard horrible date stories from someone else. And hearing other people's stories does make us feel better about our own dating disasters. So consider this book like a personal letter to you. Consider it therapy. I want you to know there is someone out there who has had it much worse than you, even if it means reliving the forty-four worst dates of my life.

After you read this, I may need to hear your horrible date stories.

THE FIRST DATE

TIM

On a balmy, breezy Friday night in the winter of 1994, I pulled up to Tim's house for our first date. I was driving my maroon 1993 Toyota Celica with the sunroof tilted up to look sporty. I drove that car around Los Angeles with the pride of a tiger. I had my car washed that day so that it would sparkle like a marquise diamond, and I had the car wash add "new car" scent air freshener, which surprisingly works.

I was looking as good as I possibly could in my black button-down shirt and faded jeans with deliberately ripped holes in the knees. I was wearing edgy sneakers to seem laid-back and hip. My hair was as spiky as I could make it. I had the confidence of a bull charging a matador's red cape.

The omnipresent Los Angeles palm trees were swaying gently in the wind, like a Las Vegas show-girl's headdress center stage. The trees appeared to dance, and the rustling branches created a sound that was soothing and relaxing. It was just windy enough to blow the smog away.

It was a very clear night—the operative word being *clear* because the air in Los Angeles is rarely clear. When the air is clear in LA, it puts true Angelenos in a great mood and almost everyone comes across as nearly friendly—almost human. Calm down, I said almost!

I had been looking forward to my date all day long. Not working the day before gave me plenty of time to go the gym, get a haircut, and drink plenty of water so that my skin looked fantastic. Unfortunately, having the day off before this date gave me way too much time to fantasize how great he might be. I was happy. I was excited. Too excited.

It took me forty-five minutes to drive six miles to Tim's house, so I really had to pee when I arrived. Going anywhere in a car in LA is quite often a mini road trip. I figured I could hold my bladder until we got to the restaurant. From the curb, Tim's house was charming, extremely well kempt, and manicured, which pleasantly surprised me.

I called Tim from my console-mounted car phone (hey, it was 1994), and he came out, looking more attractive than I remembered. The reason I didn't remember Tim well is because I had met him at a bar, and I was really drunk at the time. (So perhaps he didn't remember what I looked like also?) Oh well, too late. Whatever he remembered, as he walked toward my car, all I could think was, *This guy is hot!*

It seemed like it took him an hour to get to my car, as if he were walking in slow motion. I was thinking of so many things. *I bet he's witty, smart, good in bed. And hopefully he has a huge penis.* (Hey, let's face it; no one hopes that a guy has a small dick.)

With those visions still floating around in my head (like soap bubbles with tiny little fairy godmothers inside them), Tim opened my car door, plopped down, and before he could even close the door…he farted.

My imaginary soap bubbles quickly popped like nuclear explosions. The fairy godmothers shrieking out in horror as Tim let one rip with the roar of a ferocious lion defending its young. This was not a petite little quiet fart that easily could have been passed off as a leather seat noise, but a loud, horrendous, male fart. The kind of fart a bunch of guys watching the Super Bowl do on purpose to make each other laugh.

I didn't know what to do next. I froze up, deadpan expression, like a person on a diet caught going into the refrigerator at 2:00 a.m. Should I have pretended like I was sleepwalking?

I made the split-second decision to ignore Tim's form of nonverbal communication. At which point Tim chimed in with, "I had a bean burrito for lunch."

I was completely silent. My mouth was wide open as I stared directly ahead, my nostrils internally closed off at prison lockdown.

I had a gut feeling this night would not end well.

Tim closed the door and I thought, *Oh my god,*

how the hell do I carefully and discreetly roll down the windows? So many thoughts were going through my head. This time, my thoughts were not fantastical. I was perplexed. I was offended. And…I also thought it was funny. But I didn't know what the social filter would be for addressing a first date, first impression, first fart together.

At last I decided to ignore it and drive on. Hey, we all make mistakes, right? He was probably more embarrassed than I was.

I decided to ignore the entire incident, until…

Ten minutes later, while we were still driving to dinner, Tim leaned back, lifted up his knees with his hands, looked over at me, farted again, and said, "Take that."

I had an internal freak-out. I started wondering, *Could I sue?* He was on my leather seats, which I suddenly valued much more than I valued him. I had also gone out of my way to have my car smell like a new car. Conversely, this douche-lord was going out of his way to have my car smell like his lunch.

What a pig.

Although the date was not physically over, it was mentally over. I realized I was about to head into a parallel universe for the night where no one (except oneself) ever makes sense. Moreover, I felt like I was caught in one of those hidden-camera-show moments where the whole show is based on my reaction, except there was no camera and no show.

We went to dinner and all I could think about was—you guessed it—the fart. He was talking about his siblings, his mom, his job, and all I could hear and see and smell were a couple of big farts. They say first impressions last a lifetime, so how could we have any future together? I looked at the bright side—it was Friday night and I wasn't at home alone watching old episodes of *Bewitched* on TV Land. So instead of abandoning the date, I thought, *Two can play this game*, and I began to eat my own body weight in food. He wanted to act like a pig, so I would show him I was up for the challenge. Unfortunately, my overeating did not phase him at all.

It was clear Tim was missing a few marbles—the important ones that change the game.

I will spare you the boring dinner details. However, I did make him pay the bill.

When we got back to his place, I was prepared to come to a slow roll and push him out. However, I decided to just act civil.

I came to a stop and quickly said, "I have to wake up early." And in the middle of my sentence he had the nerve to lean in for a kiss.

I made the instantaneous decision to go ahead and let him kiss me, and I reciprocated. I thought this could be his last chance for him to make me forget about the rest of the entire evening. That didn't happen. The kiss was terrible and sloppy and wet, a little bit like what it might be like to make out with a thirsty elephant. Thankfully, the kiss did not cause him to continue with his ridiculous anal outbursts.

He got out of my car and I was happy to see him go.

Tim called me the next day and left a voicemail message: "Hey, Eddie, I had a great time last night, when are you taking me out—" I pressed the delete button as fast as I could.

I saw Tim out several weeks later at a restaurant in Los Feliz and told my friends who were with me the story. From then on we decided to always refer to him as Inflatulation.

TIM
AKA: INFLATULATION

▪■ A WORD OF WARNING

You are going to have to remind yourself that these are REAL dates I have been on. What I have to tell you in this book will seem almost *un*real, but let me assure you this is nonfiction. The stories I have to share with you are so fucking bizarre they couldn't possibly be made up. I normally hate flatulation humor, and it is ironic that I am forced to write about it. Luckily, there is no such other story in this book.

If you are searching for a happy ending, put the book down now. If you hope I end up married, put the book down now. This will not be an unrealistic Disney ending. There will be no singing and dancing furniture or candlesticks. There will be no sunset for me to walk toward, unless I am doing it by myself or it is a movie backdrop. So instead of looking for a happy ending or some glorious epiphany, just have fun and laugh. Laughter is incredible medicine.

So who the hell am I? I am in my thirties and I'm still single. (As you will find out, this is not due to lack of effort.) I'm not stupid. I pride myself on being intelligent, successful, stable, and at least somewhat attractive. I have two college degrees from the University of Southern California. My degrees are not in psychology, but I kind of wish they were so that I could figure out what the fuck is wrong with most people. Do you ever feel like you are the only person making sense on this planet? I think that at least once a day.

While I don't want it to overshadow everything else I have to tell you, I feel I must also give you a bit of background on my amazing life. And by "amazing" I mean extremely messy and plagued with all types of childhood traumas that have yet to kill me or send me into intense, never-ending therapy.

I was semi-raised on and off by my grandparents.

My grandfather once chased me around the back-yard with a shovel, telling me he was going to kill me and use the shovel to dig my grave. He was partly serious. I think. It may have been a war flashback. I found it funny.

The inspiration for his outrage that particular day was that he caught me wearing my grandmother's shoes. I didn't see anything wrong with a pair of nice, comfortable heels around the house. I don't know why he freaked out, and as I ran I started wondering if I maybe chose the pair *he* liked to wear—like I had sat in Archie Bunker's chair or something.

Other memories of my younger years jumble together in a hilariously dysfunctional blur. My child-hood included working (underage) at my grandpar-ents' fast-food restaurants in Arizona on my summer breaks while one of their adult male employees con-stantly asked me to have sex with him. And then there was the time I ran away to the bushes in our front yard for the night. And the time in third grade when I threw up on a nun in Catholic school. (Hey, she had it coming; the bitch used to hit me with a ruler. One day I grabbed it out of her hands and hit her back.) And, of course, the times when our priest used to sit me on his lap until he had an erection. It took me years to figure out what *father* kept in his pocket.

Awww, such memories of childhood. Having a prodigious sense of humor and being able to laugh at your life, and yourself, is all the therapy you might ever need. Some people stuck in the middle of a forest will crawl into a tree hole and die. I, on the other hand, will build a village, start a colony of people who speak my own language, wait for the statue of me to be built, and then exit the forest, leaving it changed forever.

Still, needless to say, I did not have the white-picket-fence childhood. And I haven't even mentioned yet that I was raised mostly in Southern California in the San Fernando Valley. The infamous Valley is home to celebrities, hippies, yuppies, and a whole gaggle of porn stars. Growing up in the porn capital of the world you have four options: (1) pretend like you are above the mere concept of porn and never watch it; (2) become a porn addict; (3) become a porn star; or (4) find porn tremendously funny and watch it while eating popcorn. I chose the latter.

Growing up in Los Angeles is like growing up in an amusement park without any rides—visually entertaining without a lot of substance. Dating in LA is even more awkward and fucked up. People wear Rolex watches they can't afford. They wear clothes they can't afford. They drive Mercedes and Porsches but they live in apartments. The grass seems so green here, but you have to remember that it's growing from dirt.

But don't get me wrong, I love Los Angeles. Where else in the world can you drive one hour in one direction and be at the beach and go the opposite direction and be snow skiing all in the same day? And where else in the world can a kid who used to wear his grandma's heels go on to land the starring role in not one but *forty-four* insanely horrible dates?

So, yes, enough about me, time to get to the dates. First, a few things you should know about the stories to follow.

All names in this book are completely fictitious. They have been changed to protect me from lawsuits that would result in my having to pay money to the dumb dicks who have already stolen precious time from my life, not to mention my hard-earned money on dinners that turned into nothing more than intestinal gas and shit. Nevertheless, the stories are real and honest.

I didn't write this book to make money. I wrote it for the billions of people who have been on horrible dates. This book is not about me, or my sexuality. This book is about the camaraderie of bad dates. It does not matter if you are straight, gay, male, female, transgender, lesbian, bi—horrible dates are universal.

Also, as you read these, keep in mind I am writing about nearly two decades of dating. I don't want you to think I am a whore who did this all in a matter of months. Also note that since the span of these dates is roughly 1994–2011, it involves everything from "old-fashioned" landline phone calls to the unexplainable overuse of texting, cell phones, and the Internet (the death of real communication).

Finally, if you have no sense of humor and can't handle curse words, you should put this fucking book down and perhaps go see *father* for a lap ride. This book requires a spectacular and twisted sense of humor. Most of what I have to write is not gorgeous, because sometimes the truth is ugly, or in this case, funny.

For everyone who can empathize and knows what it's like to be on at least one shitty date, this is for you. For everyone who wants that dinner back or sat through a boring, horrible movie only to determine that the person you were with was a complete and utter tsunami, this book is for you. If you have been completely impervious to a horrible date, then you are a perfect human being and the only person on planet Earth good enough for you is Rob Lowe (whom I am thoroughly convinced is not human. No one can age that well without selling his soul to the devil).

For everyone else, buckle your seat belt and turn off your phone, because a massive car wreck is about to begin.

THE DATES

ROGER

I met Roger when I was attending college at USC in the late 1990s. He was really stunning, with blond hair and amazing sky-blue eyes. Every time I saw him on campus, he made serious eye contact with me. I thought he was a little bit older, perhaps in grad school. But he was ridiculously hot, so who cares.

We didn't say a word to each other for months. We just kept on passing each other between classes, and clearly neither of us had the nerve to approach the other. Roger and I shared a real college innocence, and lack of confidence in our eye contact. We would question each other with our eyes. He couldn't tell why I was looking, and I wasn't sure why he was looking.

Finally, one day he got the nerve to stop me and start a conversation. I was really nervous. As he spoke, I realized he was from Germany and had a sexy accent. We talked only briefly, because we were both nervous and both had classes to get to. We exchanged cell phone numbers.

Roger and I spoke later that night on the phone. (I called right away; I don't like to play dating games.) We talked a lot. His accent was so endearing and attractive. He lived in West Hollywood, though, which was a concern for me. Guys who live in WEHO tend not to be my type. But I was open-minded, young, and naïve. Roger was a senior and I was a junior. An older man seemed like a hot idea. And he was my height, which meant if things worked out, I could double my wardrobe for free—something to seriously consider. (This can't be done in the hetero world. It's like one of the benefits of being a man: we can pee anywhere.)

It was Tuesday when we spoke on the phone and made plans for Friday night. We had several phone conversations between Tuesday and Friday and talked about superficial stuff like where each of us was from and so forth. It turned out he was an undergrad at the age of forty, which was not necessarily a problem, because a lot of people go back to school after they have worked awhile or taken care of their kids (although, in his case, he'd done neither). In addition, the problem is that forty-year-olds in Los Angeles look twenty-eight. I am convinced LA is the test city for aliens to study humanity, and the test isn't going so well.

Roger and I spoke again on Thursday night and all still seemed fine. We made plans to get dinner and go to a movie if we could fit the movie into our schedule. He said he would pick me up at 8:00 p.m.

Friday came and I was so excited. I couldn't focus all day in school. Every time one of my professors spoke, all I could hear was Roger's voice on the phone. All of a sudden, everyone on campus looked like Roger. I drove home from school with such zest and joy that going only five miles in the epic span of two hours didn't even bother me. Everything seemed better that day. The air seemed crisper. Food tasted better. I looked great, as I was glowing from the inside out with happiness.

So, the next thing I knew it was Friday, 8:30 p.m. Yeah, that's right, 8:30—and I was still sitting at home waiting for Mr. Right to show up for our 8:00 p.m. date.

No phone call.

Now, let's get something straight. There are unspoken dating rules.

Five minutes late is normal, especially in Los Angeles traffic.

Ten minutes is okay and slightly accepted.

Fifteen minutes, though, requires a cell phone call or text message.

If someone doesn't have a cell phone after the year 2000, they might not be from earth and are as un-datable as someone who wears still Ed Hardy– bedazzled clothes.

Thirty minutes late with no phone call, and you may as well not show up for the date unless you got into a car accident, the air bag went off, and you've had to spend the past twenty minutes filling out insurance papers at the hospital.

Finally, at 8:45 p.m., Roger called from the curb in front of my house and said to come out. As mad as I was, I figured, *What the hell? I need food.*

I got in the car, and he didn't even acknowledge being late. So fucking annoying. Anyway, I decided to forgive him, because he was just about the hottest person I have ever been that physically close to.

He was acting kind of rushed, fidgety, and in a frenzy, which I thought was adorable—kind of his way of nonverbally apologizing for being late. So I was prepared to start forgiving him. I would let him make it up to me by paying for dinner (which would be news to him when the bill came).

We proceeded to drive away, at which point he suggested we should just *hit a drive-thru* instead of going out to dinner, since the movie was starting at 9:30. I said nothing, because I was just trying to be easygoing, which at that time I was not. Plus, since he was late I had already eaten a brown sugar cinnamon Pop-Tart. (Okay, I really had four.)

The next thing I knew, he swiftly made a left turn and drove to an In-N-Out Burger. In all of our telephone conversations before the date, we had talked about the fact that I am a vegetarian. So, on top of everything that was about to occur, he'd never even listened to me.

I said, "What are we doing here?" He started acting rushed and jittery like when he had first picked me up. However, now he was fumbling with the radio, rolling down the windows, rolling up the windows, opening and closing the sunroof. I asked him if he was okay. He wouldn't sit still. I said, "Hello, are you okay?"

Roger then told me he had hit a bump on the way over. I said, "Oh, I'm sorry. Is that why you were late? Is your car okay; are you okay?"

He looked at me and said, "No, stupid. I said…I did a bump."

I had no idea what the hell he was talking about.

I asked him and he just looked at me. Finally I demanded he tell me what that meant.

He said, "You know, a bump, rhymes with stump," and as he said this he grabbed his crotch and then he licked his lips. Then he said, "My mouth is so dry I need a drink."

Then he burped.

Believe it or not, I still had no idea what he was talking about. What the hell was wrong with this dude?

Finally he told me I should "calm down" because a bump meant a "bump" of cocaine. And he said it with such arrogance, as if I was an idiot for not knowing what he was talking about.

So here I was, at the In-N-Out Burger drive-thru line, with a guy who was forty-five minutes late for our date, with a cocaine high in full effect, and driving me around town on drugs. So I did what anyone with no common sense and no plan, but a lot of pride and self-esteem, would do.

I got out of the car and started walking home down Sunset Boulevard.

His car was blocked in by other cars, so I knew he couldn't chase me down. I walked down Sunset with total pride, like I had just won an Olympic gold medal. He did his bump. I did the dump. Buh-bye.

Until I realized—I'd left my house keys in his car. Fuck. I had no intention of going back to grovel for my keys. I had a set of house keys hidden in the bushes at home, in a white-trash fake rock. So I kept walking.

I saw him on campus a few weeks later and walked the other direction.

To this day, I *never* leave my keys in anyone's car.

ROGER
AKA: IN-N-OUT BURGER

PIERRE

There was a great dance club/bar in Los Angeles called Hot Dog. It was always packed with an assorted crowd of hip guys, hot women in short skirts, in-shape gay guys, lesbians, transsexuals, male cross-dressers, and overall just really interesting people. The Hot Dog crowd had a great sense of humor and was one of the few bars in LA that had no attitude. Judgment and bitchiness were not an option. No one dressed to impress. No one was wearing a Rolex.

One night while at Hot Dog with two of my closest friends, Brian and Dawnne, I locked eyes with this guy across the dance floor. He was my height (five foot ten) and really cute. He had lime-green eyes that made him look like a sexy leprechaun—I could already see the pot of gold at the end of his rainbow. He had the second most beautiful eyes I had ever seen in person. (The first being this crazy Armenian guy I dated who I later found out wore colored contacts.)

This guy kept staring at me, looking away occasionally. Finally he walked over to me on the dance floor. It was loud, but I could hear his adorable accent. He was French, and he said his name was Pierre. I am a sucker for an accent!

Pierre and I hit it off immediately. Everything he said sounded better than it would in regular English because his accent and lack of correct verb usage were adorable. He was charismatic and he joined our group seamlessly—like birds flying in a *V* formation. Before I knew it, many drinks later, 2:00 a.m. arrived, much faster than I had hoped. We never even heard "last call for alcohol." Most bars in LA close at 2:00 a.m., which is a complete bummer when you feel like you can stay out all night.

So after we were forced out by some muscle-head

security goon, we were all standing around outside the club. I gave Pierre my business card, which had my cell phone number. He called my cell phone in front of me and left me a message while I was standing there: "Hi, Eddie. It's Pierre. I'm standing in front of you and you are hot." He won major points for doing that. Then Pierre gave me a little kiss good-bye, and my friends and I left.

Sunday morning I woke up thinking about how long I should play it cool waiting to call Pierre. Surprisingly, he called at 10:00 a.m. In the seconds it took for the phone to ring twice I was able to run a million thoughts through my head. *Does Pierre not know about the waiting-two-day rule? Does he not know that Sunday is the sacred ignore-the-person-you-met-the-night-before holiday?* Still, I thought it was refreshing that he had the nerve to call the next morning. So I quickly took his call.

We ended up talking for almost two hours. We talked about everything from jobs, family, religion, crazy people in LA, and a little bit about sex but with no major sex details. I found I loved his French-to-English accent even more than I had the night before.

Then, just before we hung up, he said, "I cannot believe someone like you is single."

Pierre earned special bonus points for saying that. The pinball machine lights in my head went crazy. His French charm was making me rethink my beliefs about French people—that they are all assholes.

We made plans to meet for coffee (which I don't drink) on Tuesday night. Since I am a true romantic at heart, my mind started racing: *Will I move to France? Will we get married, and can I get French citizenship? Will my sister, Lisa, like him? Will my family like him? Who will be the breadwinner? Who will stay home to raise the kids? Who gets the Jeep? Who gets the sports car? Can I go two days until I see him again?*

Monday we didn't speak. Tuesday morning I sent him a text message to confirm our date. He texted back, "I am excited see you," and he also texted me his address. Abbreviated texts bug the shit out of me. I was pleased when Pierre spelled out his entire text message, and his lack of correct English just seemed to further avalanche into a pile of amazing adorableness.

All day Tuesday seemed to take forever. Isn't it odd how slowly a clock ticks when you want something to occur? And how fast a clock ticks when you *don't* want something to occur?

Finally 8:00 p.m. arrived and I was in front of his apartment building. He lived in a very nice building—a 1920s Spanish building in the historic area of Los Angeles called Miracle Mile. The building was gorgeous, with great detail, and I could just imagine the amazing parties that were held there back in the day. Where someone lives says a lot about his or her personality.

He came out, and he looked adorable and preppy and really clean. Don't you love it when people look clean? I don't understand the dirty grunge look. I also don't understand guys wearing jeans below their asses. Really fucking annoying.

We talked in the car with the same great energy as the phone call we had Sunday morning. We arrived at the Coffee Bean on Third Street, ordered drinks, and sat outside. As we sat, I realized that he was even hotter than I'd thought he was when I was drunk. While I was thinking that, he said, "You look hotter than I remember." I thought, *Oh my god, we are going to fall in love.* My thought bubble also contained the two of us on the bow of the *Titanic.* I was Leo. He was Kate. And our ship would not sink!

We talked nonstop for hours until the employees came out and said they were closing down. Pierre was smart. He was funny. He had a great body. He loved his family. This was one of the best dates I had ever been on. It wasn't based on some sassy over-priced meal and formal attire. It was laid-back, relax-ing, and stimulating—a rare combination. And to top it off, Pierre also said he was about to become a U.S. citizen, so all our ducks were in a row to live happily ever after.

So I thought.

We left the Bean, got in my car, and drove back to his place. When we pulled up, he asked me to park and come up for a little while. I thought, *Perfect, his apartment will be filthy and hideous and I can stop liking him so much.*

Pierre held my hand all the way up to his apartment, not caring who looked at us. (Most European people have much less insecurity about sexual identity.) He was scoring so many points that if this were a video game, he would already be at Level 10, have a million points, and four spare lives. If I were Pacman, and he were a ghost, I would let him catch me and eat me.

When he opened the door to his apartment, I was extremely disappointed.

His apartment was beautiful and immaculate. You could eat off the floors. I was disappointed because I still had no ammunition to load my normal disappointment gun, and I wasn't used to that. He had amazing taste, great artwork, and true mid-century furniture. I could move right in and live with him forever. I kept thinking to myself, *What the hell is this guy doing single?*

Little did I know I was about to find out at least *one* reason why he was single.

We sat down on his couch. He went to the kitchen and came back with a bottle of red wine. I love red wine. Before I knew it, we were opening a second bottle. I am a super lightweight.

The next thing I knew, we were making out. Somehow we had made our way into his bedroom. On our way, our clothes were getting ripped off and thrown all over his immaculate apartment. His body was "sick" hot. He had no body fat, eight-pack abs, and a bubble butt that I could have rested my drink on.

We finally made it to the bed and the sexual heat was on full blast. We rolled around naked, and our swords were headed into full battle. He kept aiming my sword toward his bubble butt, so we were completely compatible. I remember thinking, *How could this get any better? What will our next date be like? Is this just sex? Is this a date? Oh fuck I need to lose weight.*

As I was getting lost in thought, Pierre said, "Do you wanna have some more fun?…Hold on, I'll be right back." He then ran into the kitchen, naked, as I watched his amazing butt scurry into the next room.

I sat back, thinking, *Holy shit, if he gets any more alcohol I will probably upchuck all over his spotless bedroom*.

I heard him rustling around in the fridge. Shit. How in the hell was I going to be able to drink any more wine?

A few seconds later Pierre came back into the room…just as I was realizing that red wine is typically not kept in a fridge.

He just stood at the bedroom door, staring at me.

I said, "Did you get some more wine…where is it?" He seemed to be trying to get up the nerve to speak. After he spoke, I realized why he'd been hesitating.

Pierre pulled out the hand that was hidden behind his back. He opened the hand, which I immediately saw was holding a hot dog. He said: "Stick this in me."

I was dead silent.

Was this a joke? Was this a test? Is this really happening?

I sobered up fast. I sprang up from the bed like a kid on Christmas morning. Santa, however, had nothing to do with this. So I got dressed, and left.

I drove home so disappointed. Hey, I don't mind a few freaky moments here and there in the bedroom, but, seriously, on a first date? How was I ever going to look him in the face again without seeing a hot dog? How would I ever look a hot dog in the face again?

I drove home thinking, *Oh my god, the name of the bar is Hot Dog. Is there some type of connection? Does everyone there stick hot dogs up their asses? Does everyone there assume that I stick hot dogs up my ass? Should I have brought some relish, ketchup, and mustard?* It was really hard to fall asleep that night.

The next morning I did what any sane person would do. I called my best friend, Matthew, to tell him the story. Matthew is the most intelligent person I have ever known or met, but he also has a wicked sense of humor, so I knew he would put it all in perspective. I also knew he would greatly appreciate the story.

Matthew managed to make me feel better. "I highly doubt the bar Hot Dog is in cahoots with Oscar Mayer," he said. "I highly doubt anyone else in that bar is cramming hot dogs up one another's asses. No, people in France are not known for doing that. Pierre sounds like a total freak, and the fact that his house is beautiful and perfect and that he's hot is irrelevant. You will never be able to look at a hot dog the same way again. Move on."

I took everything Matthew said into consideration. I usually do exactly as he says, because he is pragmatic, insightful, and always has my best interests at heart. He is my Gayle King.

Pierre had the common sense to not call me again, as my lightning-bolt/Flash Gordon exit was all the communication we needed. I saw him two weeks later at the same club. Before, I had seen a cute guy. Now all I could see was a huge hot dog swaying on the dance floor.

**PIERRE
AKA: HOT DOG**

STEVE

I met Steve at a dark little hole-in-the-wall bar in Silverlake, which is just north of downtown Los Angeles. Silverlake is known for eclectic people, artists, leather-daddy gays, lesbians, and yuppies renovating overpriced, tiny old houses. Steve was none of the above.

He was tall and athletic, which is a weakness of mine. He had short, thick, dark, spiky hair, which is a weakness of mine.

We talked for about two hours in the bar, which, in a bar environment, is a serious commitment. I got the vibe that he just wanted to go home and fuck all night long, but I kind of liked him. So I decided we would just exchange numbers, and that way I could get him to take me on a real date. However, I apparently forgot to ask something that I never should have had to ask.

I called him the next day, which is taboo and frowned upon by all players in the Sunshine State and by most single people in general. But I figured, *Why the hell not*?

So after leaving him a message, I was delightfully surprised when he called right back. Was this my *next* Mr. Right? Would neither of us play any dating games? Was I finally on the same page as someone else? Had I found my soul mate at a bar? Would I move to his place? Would he move to my place? How would it all come together? I answered the call filled with first-date excitement but managed to keep it cool. I began to speak slowly, and cool—neither of which are my personality.

"Hey, Steve, what's up?"

There was a long, awkward silent pause.

Then, in a hurry, Steve said, "Well, I just wanted to call you right back [pause again]…to tell you I'm married, but if you want to hook up…"

I hung up the phone. I felt like he had just rubbed a lemon on my asshole to make it pucker and feel like it was on fire. *Hey, assholes, if you are married, don't lead us single people on by giving us your phone number. Leave us single people the hell alone.*

Exchanging phone numbers with people who are interested in you should only happen if you are *single*. Anyone who only gives the illusion they are single need not apply. If I wanted to just go out and get fucked, we would have gone home together that night. Right? That douche should have been wearing a ring!

**STEVE
AKA: THE RING OF FIRE**

Dave

My friend Lou said he knew a guy named Dave who was perfect for me. Turns out he was not.

Why is it that all of your friends think they have the perfect person for you and in reality that person could not be any worse for you? Either your friends have a really fucked-up perception of who you really are, or they just don't know you at all, or they think a lot less of you than you realize.

Anyway, Lou said Dave was a comedian and we should go see him perform some Saturday night.

Having done some stand-up comedy in my past, I had a few concerns.

I don't date WAMs (waiter-actor-models), which also includes TBFs (trying to be famous). Not only do I not date them, but I don't even want any of them as friends. I realize that, living in Los Angeles, that rules out a lot of people, but after living here all my life I'm okay with that! However, I forgot to rule out comedians. I forgot that comedians most likely want to be famous also. All I was thinking about was that since *I* am so ridiculously funny, a comedian might be the perfect fit for me.

So we went to see Dave perform. The comedy club was in the basement of a crappy little Moroccan restaurant on Melrose, so I assumed I had nowhere to go with him but up. The interior of this restaurant looked like Middle Eastern throw up—with tassels and drapes. I suppose it should have been a sign.

Still, Dave was great, the best performer of the night by far. He was seriously good looking (a rare trait in comedians). He had a great energy about him (or so I thought), and I decided I wanted to meet him.

After his performance Lou and I met him backstage. We chatted a little, and there was instant chemistry. I gave him my phone number.

Dave called me the next day. He wanted to go out that night for a drink, and he made it clear that he meant it as a date. I told him I would meet him wherever he wanted to go. He wanted to go to this little bar on Melrose. I thought, *Melrose again?* Okay.

He said he liked to go to straight bars and didn't go to gay bars. He was already winning some points. People who step outside their comfort zone or think outside the box earn major points with me! Life is short, so make it interesting.

We met at 9:00 p.m. for drinks. The bar was crowded and noisy, which to me is the perfect environment for a date, because there's not the added pressure of a stuffy, silent, catatonic restaurant. He was engaging. And funny. His chances were improving. We plowed through a couple drinks like two dehydrated camels at a pond. I was buzzed. He was buzzed.

The conversation was going great, but I didn't feel like I was finding out much about him. So I asked, "Where are you from?"

And here is where it all went wrong in one sentence.

Steve stood up silently. Then he pretended to push his penis between his legs, crossed his legs, pointed to his crotch and said: "I am from my mother's cunt."

I was in utter shock, and at a complete loss for words.

First of all, that's not even original material. Second, almost every twelve-year-old boy has done that at some point in his life while naked and in front of a mirror. (For those men who say they have never done that, I am here to tell you, yes they have.) I guess he was just trying to be shocking. But all I got was shock-based aversion therapy, because I was thoroughly turned off. It's one thing to do that with a friend after you've had too many margaritas and in the privacy of your own home. It's another thing if that's the first glimpse you get of someone's personality.

Being unsure how I would speak to him after that event, I decided to say nothing. I thought, *Never enable bad joke tellers, and, more importantly, never enable bad comedians.*

I wasn't drunk enough to handle this date.

From that point on, I tried my best to ignore

everything he did and said. I started to point out other hot guys so he would realize we were done. I ordered another drink. I had once read that if you try to get drunk to avoid something, it takes twice as long. But I assumed I was doomed either way. Nothing he did or said was funny anymore. His bad joke made him look really ugly all of sudden.

Thirty minutes later I deliberately yawned and declared I was really tired and told him I had to go. When he offered to walk me to my car, I told him I had walked, which was a lie. I left vowing to remove his horrible joke from my brain. I could not. It made a lifelong impression that I wish I could extract from my brain.

Then I went home and ate a banana and a grape Popsicle to regain balance in my life. Food is always reliable and you know what to expect.

I never spoke to Dave again. And neither should his mother!

**DAVE
AKA: MY MOTHER'S WHO-HA**

⬜ RICH

I was shopping at Ralph's Grocery store on Ventura Boulevard in Studio City. It was just an ordinary day, and I was minding my own business looking for my normal staple supplies: canned tuna, fruit, etc. I saw this guy who seemed really attractive from a distance, but I didn't give it much thought. I don't eat beef, so I would not be shopping for any in a grocery store.

As I went up and down several aisles, though, I realized the same guy kept appearing.

I wondered if maybe the grocery store had hired him to entertain me while I shopped.

At first I thought it was coincidence, until I realized there were only two items in his hand-held basket. He was really attractive up close, and I was flattered that he would go out of his way to get my attention, so I just said hi, very noncommittal and butch-like. He said hi back and we both kept walking. I'm not sure why I didn't stop and talk. I think because I got nervous. Attraction to another person can often produce very strange behavior.

When I was at the checkout stand, I looked around for my grocery store lover, but he was nowhere to be found. I assumed he thought I wasn't attractive. Or worse, he might be straight. (You would be *really* shocked at how many straight guys check out other guys, and it often does not mean anything.) I continued to go through the checkout stand, really taking my time, hoping to get one last glimpse of my grocery store lover, but he wasn't around. I thought, *How dare he stalk me and then disappear? How rude!*

After checking out and paying for my groceries, I walked to my car. Lo and behold, there was my lover standing there with his one bag of groceries.

He now earned the title Grocery Store Stalker. Yet, I was impressed with his resilience and dedication.

I was nervous, but I rolled my cart up to him and we started talking. His name was Rich, and I could tell right away he wasn't the sharpest crayon in the box. I think the muscles in his body were putting too much pressure on his head and causing poor blood circulation to his brain. He was really hot, so I was ignoring the fact that we would probably end up having nothing in common. I remained open-minded. You must remain open in life to let new things in.

He ripped off a piece of his grocery store bag and wrote his number on it, which I thought was endearing and creative. I took his number and then told him I had to go because I needed to get my groceries home. I walked away feeling surprised and pleased that I had ended up meeting him. One of the great things about being a guy who likes guys—guys will make the first move, so there are two people willing to make the first move. I hereby encourage all women to go ahead and make the first move.

I called Rich later that day and asked if he wanted to meet me for coffee. I am a huge fan of meeting for coffee as a date. It is the perfect environment to decide if you want to commit to a dinner. It gives you a chance to get a sense of what someone might be like. You can tell a lot about a person by the way they order at Starbucks or Coffee Bean. Complicated order, complicated person!

Anyway, we met at the Coffee Bean next to that same Ralph's. When he arrived, he looked less attractive for some reason. I probably did also, so I didn't really care.

I tried sparking conversation, but it was like talking to a Muppet without the hand up its ass. Ever try to talk to a stuffed animal? The eyes might move, but nothing comes out of the mouth. He did tell me several times I had a great ass and I was hot, but that's really all he kept saying. I realized he didn't want a date, he just wanted sex. And he was really dumb, dropped-on-his-head-as-an-infant dumb.

I told Rich I had to get up really early, which was a lie. It is okay to make social, shallow lies, but please do not lie about anything important. He asked if

I wanted to come back to his place, which I knew would lead to sex.

I hadn't had sex with anyone other than myself in almost a year, so I said yes.

Okay, I'll stop you right there. I don't sleep around and I'm not a whore. But I do think sex is natural and healthy. We Americans are way too repressed about sexuality. When I was in Italy in 2001, I saw a billboard of a woman showing her breasts and the advertisement was for toothpaste. If I were straight, I would move to Italy just for the billboards. My point—relax people, it's just sex…and nudity.

We drove back to Rich's apartment in Studio City. The building was a total dump. His apartment was furnished with white plastic outdoor furniture from Goodwill and a TV on the floor. I am not compatible with messy people or adults who don't own a single thing. How could anyone get by in life owning nothing? This furthered my certainty that Rich and I would never have a relationship. So I figured I would make the best of the night.

So I just slept with him…on his mattress…that was on the floor.

Don't judge me, we have all slept with someone who had a mattress on the floor!

Okay, I actually slept with him two times—once that night and once again a week later. He was really good in bed.

But man was he dumb. I usually reserve the word *dumb* for movies, bad jokes, Dalmatians, and Regis Philbin. Calling a person dumb is just about the worst thing you can say. But Rich is really dumb. Once I brought up Tipper Gore, and he thought Tipper Gore was a male professor at Santa Monica College. I'm not kidding.

After that I never called him again. If you have nothing in common with someone, you have no future!

Cleanup on aisle four.

RICH
AKA: GROCERY STORE STALKER

◼◼ WALTER

This was another one of those fix-ups. You know, when a great friend has the "perfect" person for you. This date was like one of those odd compliments you get from a stranger: "You look just like Jennifer Aniston, except she is taller, has different color eyes, and different hair." It's what I call a "hubcap compliment." A reflection from a hubcap distorts everything, and so do compliments like that. This date was a *hubcab*.

Walter was a lawyer and I met him at a friend's dinner party at a multi-million dollar house on the famous Mulholland Drive. The house was amazing, with an entire panoramic view of Los Angeles. You could see all the way from downtown to the beach.

Being that high up, we could also see stars in the sky. The view was so spectacular that I think I was in a trance and my judgment was skewed. I also had a lot to drink.

I talked with Walter most of the night. When you commit to talking to one person you've just met at a party, it sends a real message. Usually when you start to talk to someone, most people know right away whether they are interested or not.

I was interested and so was Walter.

Walter was stable and owned a house. Owning an actual house, with a yard, in Los Angeles is like being from another planet. But it was a planet I wanted to visit right away. We hit it off instantly, as if we were the only two people at the party. I was excited to get to know him. Everything seemed to fit into place. He was G.D.—*geographically desirable*. He had a career. He had a car. He appeared to like me a lot. He put his arm around me on the deck overlooking the city. The pieces were fitting together as easily as a child's four-piece puzzle.

Our first date was dinner, and it was enjoyable, at a nice restaurant with great food. Great food is often equal to great sex! Our second date was a movie, and the movie was good so the date seemed decent. Our third date was dinner at the beach, and it was romantic. We walked on the beach at night after dinner, and he gave me his jacket. I know it sounds like some kind of movie bullshit, but that's exactly what happened, and it was magical and special and I was starting to like him. Most importantly, we had not had sex by this point. We had only kissed and managed a little over-the-pants groping in the car.

We ended up going on four above average dates and I was getting mentally prepared for the fifth date to include sex. Four dates in Los Angeles without sex is like having a peanut butter and jelly sandwich without the bread—unheard of.

I was starting to get worried that maybe he had a really small penis or that maybe he wasn't sexually attracted to me. Even worse, what if I wasn't attracted to him? I had to know, so I started to plot and plan how the fifth date would involve nudity… and sex.

For our fifth date I wanted to make it special. I felt it was my turn to pay, since on all the prior dates he had refused to let me pay. I took him to a restaurant on Robertson that claims it's "Beverly Hills–adjacent," but it's really in West Hollywood. The term *adjacent* in LA (and in real estate) refers to a much nicer city than the actual city something is located in. It's a term used to trick property buyers and people who live too far away to go visit. It's like me saying my body is "amazing–adjacent." My body is not amazing, but it is in the nearby hood.

Anyway, Walter and I had a great meal. We had great conversation. And all I kept thinking about through dinner was, *Am I going to get laid by someone I actually might really like on several levels?*

We downed a few martinis at dinner. We both really started to share, talk, and open up. It was one of the best dates I had ever been on. A real spark was ignited between us—mentally and physically. I even

had fantasies about entering the dangerously affec-
tionate, cook-at-home phase of dating and how that
would play out.

Scary thoughts!

We got back to his place around midnight. As
soon as we walked in the door, we started frantically
ripping our clothes off each other, as if they were
on fire. He ruined one of my favorite shirts. By the
time we got to the bedroom, I was completely naked
and ready to go. He told me to lie on the bed. My
feet were dangling off the side. I felt so free. I felt
so naked and so comfortable being naked. I was so
relaxed. And just then…

Walter started making out with my feet. French-
kissing my feet with his tongue. And then his teeth
got invited to the party—but not by me.

Now, he began macking on my feet in a sexual way.
It quickly became aggressive and scary. He was sucking my feet and moaning the way people do when
they eat really amazing barbecued ribs. He started
biting my feet and gnawing on them with his teeth.

I just looked up at his ceiling and did my best to check out mentally.

I also really had to do my best not to laugh as my feet are very ticklish.

I thought, *Maybe this could be kind of hot. Maybe I am so out of touch that this is in. I don't remember seeing this on Oprah, though.*

Then he yelled out, "Toe jam, HOT!" Then, within a few seconds he yelled, "I just came."

I was in such shock that I couldn't move or speak.

I was frightened into speechlessness and immobility.

I was grossed out. I was pissed off.

First of all, I have never had toe jam in my life. It was probably sock debris. Second, it was not hot.

As I looked down at the guy who had just finished sucking the skin off of my toes and feet, I realized that my precious little piglets had been raped.

Those little piggies would never go to the market again.

As if that weren't bad enough, he then verbally

reminded me, "I just came all over my floors, how hot!"

Not only did this idiot not pay any attention to the fact that this entire incident made me go limp, he also didn't even care that I didn't get off. What a prick! If someone doesn't care if you get off during sex, they either don't care about you, they are too lazy, or they are too self-involved. Either way, you are doomed!

I leaned up and told him I had to go. I got up and got dressed. He walked me to the front door and tried to kiss me good-bye. I leaned back to avoid the kiss and just gave him a big hug and pat on the back.

I never spoke to him again.

Every time I see my feet now, I apologize to them. They didn't deserve that.

WALTER
AKA: THE FOOT RAPER

Ben

We met at a kid's birthday party for my friend's son. She told me he was single and looking. I love meeting people at parties, but this was a stretch even for me. A kid's birthday party, seriously? Nonetheless, most single people often go to parties hoping to meet someone new. They won't tell you that, but it's true.

We talked a few times amongst all the adolescent commotion. He seemed nice and smart. We seemed to hit if off rather well. I thought we would look great together if we dated. Looking good together is just an added bonus. It is like the cherry on top of the dating cake.

We exchanged numbers at the end of the day.

Ben seemed really laid-back and easygoing. Not many people in Los Angeles are, either.

We spoke on the phone a couple times that week. We went on a date the following Friday night to dinner in Santa Monica, where he lived. If a man devotes a Friday night to you for a date, he might really like you.

I drove to his place because my apartment was a wreck and I was too lazy to clean it just for a date. I walked up to his apartment to pick him up for dinner. He opened the door and gave me a quick peck on the lips. Then, unfortunately, he started talking.

His breath smelled like he had licked a public toilet from a truck stop. I tried to ignore it. All through dinner I kept thinking how bad his breath was and wondering if he had a missing tooth or decay. I knew I could never kiss him without gagging.

I wondered why I hadn't noticed this before, but it was irrelevant.

On the car ride home I kept the window down, because his bad breath was permeating the car. It was like the cloud of dust that surrounds the *Peanuts* character Pigpen. His breath was singeing my eyebrows. I was trying not to bring anything up that would cause conversation.

I quickly dropped him off and never called him again. He called me and left a message as I was driving home. I don't know what the message said, because I deleted it.

Now listen…

I know we all have bad breath now and then, but horrid breath like that was unforgettable. If you are going to be unforgettable on a date, do so by being amazing. If you are going to have horrid breath, do so after someone already likes you.

BEN
AKA: POTTY MOUTH

▪◾ BILL

I am going to start by giving you Bill's bio, because on paper he is the perfect catch. On paper he reads like the Declaration of Dating Independence. Off paper, and in person, Bill is a real tragic mess.

Bill has an executive position for a very well-known beverage company. He is educated, smart, witty, and has beautiful curly, thick hair. He is six foot two, slightly hairy, and a real head-turner. He looked a little bit like a Disney Prince Charming but without the pointy nose, and clearly without the damsel on his side.

What I remember most about Bill after seeing him naked for the first time: a shaved chest and shaved balls, which is borderline bizako (bizarre + wacko). Seeing shaved balls on a grown man makes him look like he is ten years old, but only from the waist down. However, it was about to get worse.

Bill had his pubic hair shaved to form an image. I was unsure exactly what the image was, and I wasn't willing to bring it up or have it become part of a conversation. I've seen letters, shapes, and numbers (yes, numbers, I have seen it) in funny porn movies, but in reality it's a BIG TURNOFF. It's not edgy. It's not trendy. It's not neat or interesting. It's gross. I don't need to be reading anything while I'm down there. Besides, I get enough reading on the streets of Los Angeles from all the personal license plates and the parking signs that require an interpreter and a Google search for definition. So the last things I need in bed are diagrams or directions. I know what to do and how to find it, usually.

Anyway, Bill and I met at a grocery store in North Hollywood. The grocery store advertisements said it was Toluca Lake–adjacent, but no matter where it wanted to be, it was in North Hollywood.

Bill was eyeing me and deliberately shopping in aisles where he wasn't putting anything into his cart.

Sound familiar? (Here's a hint: if you're going to stalk someone in the grocery store, pretend to actually be buying groceries; you'll seem a lot less creepy.) I always find it endearing and refreshing to see someone try to get my attention on the few instances it happens. So I took my time reading boxes and looking at labels of items very intensely. This grocery store lover wasn't going to get away, and he couldn't be as dumb as the other one.

I finished my shopping and couldn't see my blond prince anywhere. Déjà vu. Oh well, another life opportunity passed.

While pushing my cart down the parking lot and dodging the drivers who aim for people, I saw him again. He was waiting in his car pretending to check his cell phone, rolling down the windows, and so forth. It does not take all that time and energy to accomplish those tasks, but it was sweet nonetheless. So I glanced over and smiled. He smiled. I started to put my groceries in my trunk, the whole time thinking, *Okay, idiot, now is the time, get over here.*

He finally came over. We talked about really mundane things…names, where do you live? Blah… blah…We exchanged numbers. I asked him if he was single (something I do all the time now). He was single. As previously mentioned, I don't normally get my "meat" where I don't get my meat, but again I thought, *What the hell?*

A tad over two months later (the between story is irrelevant), we were entering a different phase of dating. It seemed to get more serious. We had a lot of sex. We had hours upon hours of conversations. Dinners, movies, a few parties, friends met him, etc.

One night at dinner, almost three months into dating, he decided to finally tell me he had oral and genital herpes that he got from an ex who cheated on him. The same ex was also suing him over things they bought together like furniture, a car, and other stuff.

OY! It was just too much information.

I was dumbfounded by his ability to keep such a secret that was pivotal to my health.

I realized he could not be trusted. And, more

importantly, I don't want the gift that keeps on giving—herpes!

I couldn't wait to make a doctor's appointment. It suddenly dawned on me. His pubic hair had so much time and attention paid to it because there was a lot of traffic down there.

I went to the doctor that week and got tested for everything…

And Bill is really lucky I didn't get his herpes. I mean, I am really lucky!

I can forgive a lot of things, but there are some things I can't forgive. After months of dating, you should not be finding out vital information about someone that can affect you. The vital information should be offered up early in the dating process. Perhaps a nice note shaved into your pubic hair: "Herpes below."

BILL
AKA: GROCERY STORE HERPES

Kevin

I met Kevin at the mall, which should have been a warning sign, as I can't stand going to malls.

I was eating in the food court. He sat near me. I noticed him and thought he was attractive, but didn't think much of it and kept eating. Soon I could feel someone staring at me. You know that creepy feeling? I looked over and Kevin was staring at me. He smiled at me. He had a shaved head and was dressed very well. In fact, he was dressed so well I felt underdressed.

He was not creepy at all.

He was wearing form-fitting dress clothes and he had a great body.

I smiled and looked back down at my food as if

something really interesting was occurring on my plate. I looked over at him a few times and he at me. He finished eating first, emptied his remaining food into the trash, placed the tray on top of the trash can, and started walking my way. He came over and said hi. I was sort of shocked. I am still always shocked when a guy has the balls to come over and say hi to me.

If anyone ever says hi to you, even if you have no interest, just say hi back.

He seemed very nice and had a great face—clean-shaven, great bone structure, smooth clear skin, and full, red lips. He was really short—I don't normally like "pocket gays," or "mini-gays," but many years of dating were lowering my standards. I hardly had any standards at all at this point. He said he was in a hurry and asked if he could get my number. We exchanged cell phone numbers.

We spoke on the phone that night. He was single. I asked.

He seemed intelligent. He lived in the Valley, as did I. He was only a few years older than me. He was saving to buy a house. He was close to his family. Everything seemed great and we made plans to go on a date.

At a certain stage in your life you must learn to ask more questions about people…

Kevin picked me up on a Friday night in his brand-new BMW. Friday night dates can be dicey, because you might not have enough energy from working all week to be "on your game." But I had a good feeling about the night. He said we were going to drive to Malibu Beach and eat on the water.

Picture an overcast and chilly night in Malibu, drinks, dinner, the ocean, waves crashing thunderously in the background, and the infinite water view. It all seemed so romantic. At dinner Kevin ordered a drink. And another…and another. I was getting concerned, because I don't get in the cars of drunk drivers.

As he drank more and more, he was getting belligerent and a lot less attractive. You have to be really drunk to tolerate other really drunk people! And then, on our first date…On our first date Kevin had the nerve to ask me if I prefer to be on the top or the bottom during sex.

He then proceeded to tell me he is NEVER on the bottom. Then he said worse things that would make this book illegal to publish—really gross sexual things that I thought only Asian circus girls could do.

He kept on proclaiming he was a *top*, and it was such a huge turnoff.

Drunk and horny are two super-ugly traits on a person for a first date.

They are perfect conditions for sex, but not a date.

Do drinks bring out the real person, or does the real person just start drinking and share too much?

I made an excuse to go to the bathroom and instead walked outside to call a cab from my cell phone. That cab ride home from Malibu to the Valley cost me forty-five dollars.

About an hour after I left, Kevin texted me: "You're an asshole...you're not even cute...I better not see you out..."

I have never seen Kevin anywhere in LA since,

and I'm not worried that I will. The fact that LA is extremely spread out and overpopulated allows you to go years, or perhaps forever, without seeing people you don't want to see. One of the benefits of a city poorly designed.

KEVIN
AKA: ANGRY BOTTOM

▪▫ VINCE

I met young, twenty-one-year-old Vince at the car wash through some flirting glances and a few smiles. He was extremely handsome. In a classic way. Like a Ralph Lauren countryside model. He had classic all-American features and great skin. We were both waiting for our cars to be finished. We were sitting in the outdoor waiting area, where everyone was wearing hats and sunglasses and texting on their phones. It is ironic that so many people here go out of their way to cover up when the weather is usually spectacular. I know a lot of people wouldn't have noticed Vince. Most people would have noticed his Porsche. I, on the other hand, have seen many of my high school classmates drive Porsches and Mercedes (except me). I couldn't have cared less what type of car he was driving. Actually, I would have preferred he be in a more working class car. Nonetheless, we carefully, and discretely, shared glances.

After an awkward final smile, he finally came over to me and said, "Hey, how's it going?" He seemed really sweet and normal. Clearly he wasn't shy, and that was a huge turn-on, as most people I see out appear to be shy. Confidence, but not cockiness, is a turn-on. We talked for a few moments and I gave him my business card.

He called that night around 10:00 p.m. WOW. No games? He asked me out to dinner the following Monday night. That worried me, as guys who ask you out on a Monday night are probably busy fucking other people on Friday and Saturday night. (ATTENTION EVERYONE: if someone only dates you on a Monday night, they don't really like you.) But I thought Vince was sweet and interesting, so I wanted to have dinner with him.

I was pleasantly surprised when he picked me

up on time. Being on time is an advantage in every situation. When he came to my door, I noticed he was dressed fairly snazzy with his Rolex watch, and now with a sassy diamond stud in his ear, which was screaming midlife crisis, and tacky. He was wearing expensive dress shoes and an expensive-looking shirt. I thought, *I must be one hot bitch if he dressed to impress*, because at the car wash he had looked so ordinary and refreshingly simple. Still, he seemed a bit over the top, since I don't wear expensive shoes, nor do I own a Rolex or a diamond earring. Nevertheless, I didn't care too much at first, as long as he didn't start acting pretentious. As the years were ticking by, my dating standards were sinking like a vented canoe with no oars, but had they sunk this low?

One of the first things Vince asked when he came into my house was if I liked his new watch. As it happens, my sister and brother own a coin business and deal in high-end jewelry and watches, so a Rolex was a recent area of expertise for me. I do love the design of Rolex watches. Unfortunately, Mr. Porsche was wearing a *fake* Rolex (a Folex). I thought, *My god, what a total douche-lord*. There are few things worse than someone wearing a fake Rolex watch. So I assumed he was also wearing cubic zirconium in his ear. I was also assuming the Porsche, fake Rolex, and gaudy earring were making up for something he was lacking—a grown-up-size penis perhaps?

We were still in my house before leaving for dinner, and I was starting to realize I had made a mistake. Again! What kind of future would I have with this douche? Would we need Louis Vuitton wallets and Tiffany key chains? Now, don't get me wrong, I love the finer things in life. I could easily become a spoiled divo (male diva) in a heartbeat. But I am not ostentatious. I like mutts over purebreds. I like cheap food over expensive food. I prefer to walk anywhere I can versus driving. I don't need to have my Braque du Bourbonnais dog named Mimi walked by the butler. I am more likely to be the butler! Please, people, let us have some perspective.

I asked Vince if he wanted a drink, because I realized I was going to need to be drunk for this date. After I asked I thought, *If this ass asks me for cognac or an apricot sour, I will lose it.*

Fortunately for me, he asked for some water. Now, no one in LA drinks tap water, not even me; everyone drinks bottled water. So, just to piss him off, I deliberately gave him tap water, to see if he would drink it. He drank the tap water. I was pleased to see he didn't care about the water, and I thought maybe I had jumped the gun in judging him.

I realigned my thoughts.

Could Vince be an okay guy? What does he like? What does he hate? Does he care about people? Would he ever do charity work with me? Does he contribute to society? Has he ever been in love? Has anyone ever loved him? Vince's drinking the tap water threw me off base. I wanted to get to know more about him just in case I was wrong. I am wrong about a lot of things on a daily basis, and this could have been one of those times.

We left for dinner. He drove us in his fancy-pants Porsche.

We ended up at a hip little restaurant/bar in Hollywood. I could tell Vince didn't have much to say when, during dinner, he blurted out, "Did I ever tell you about the time I was in Saint Barts?"

How could he have *ever* told me anything? We just met.

He said a lot more after that, but as soon as he said the words "Saint Barts," I was once again assured he was a total douche. I don't think to this day I have ever met anyone else who started a conversation with, "Did I ever tell you about the time I was in Saint Barts?" I turned my imaginary hearing aid to silent.

Vince kept talking. I tuned him out. He swiftly became Charlie Brown's teacher, and all I could hear was "WA WA WA WA WA…WA WA…WA WA."

I thought of everything I could to shut Vince out of my cognitive thoughts. I started thinking about Final *Jeopardy* questions I knew the answers to (not many). I started to think about my grocery list. I started to wonder if I had already separated my darks and my whites. I pretended to be the First Lady and just smiled a lot in his direction. I thought about naked sailors. I wondered how long it takes a snail to go a mile. I wondered how many dimples were on a golf ball. (Don't Google it; it's 300–450 depending on the type of ball.)

Meanwhile, the waiter passed by back and forth several times waiting for Mr. Folex to shut the fuck up. Finally the waiter stopped and took our orders. I ordered a chicken salad and a martini. I wanted to order a muzzle, for Vince, and a transporter, for me, with a side order of "get me the hell out of here." Vince ordered two appetizers, lobster, several martinis, and dessert. Then throughout our boring dinner, filled with conversation about places he had been and things he had bought and homes he owned, Vince ordered more martinis. I wanted to order a bottle of vodka with a funnel, or a beer in a paper bag, but I restrained myself.

Interestingly enough, and thankfully as well, the

rest of the dinner went okay for me. His nonsensical ramblings gave me plenty of mental time to plan out my weekend—without him.

When I finally got the chance to talk, I made light, stupid conversation so I would appear dumb and uninteresting. "What kind of chips do you like? I love barbecue Lays. I wonder who invented crosswalk signs?"

Somewhere in the middle of my idiotic rants, Saint Barts mentioned he was a high roller in Vegas. My parents live in Las Vegas, so when he said that, I figured we could discuss Vegas and at least that would be interesting. The conversation took a slight turn for the better, as we had seen a lot of the same shows. I am a huge fan of Cirque du Soleil and so was he. I started to think I had some commonalities with Vince. I thought, *Oh shit, might I be a douche too*?

My dinner with Vince was developing into a unique experience for me. I felt a strange attraction and revulsion toward him at the same time, which I found difficult to reconcile. I almost started to think that perhaps

I could take Vince on as a project, like a fixer-upper home with good bones but bad everything else.

Finally, after about an hour and a half of mixed conversation—some good, some bad—the bill came. Vince grabbed it. I then realized he was going to take care of the bill, and I appreciated that. It was the right thing to do, since he had invited me to dinner and took me to a place that was expensive. Besides, I'd only had a chicken salad and one drink while he feasted like a ye-olde-times king.

That's when he flipped open the leather bill folder, examined the bill for one second, turned it toward me, and said, "We each owe eighty dollars!"

I was in shock. The nerve. The gall. Now I was certain—Vince was a total idiot.

I don't know about you, but I have never had an eighty-dollar chicken salad. And how is it that he could afford a Porsche, a Folex, and a diamond earring but couldn't pick up the tab when dinner was his idea? I started to wonder if he was a con artist, a control freak, or just plain nuts. I quickly reminded myself I didn't care about him at all and I should stop psychoanalyzing him.

So, knowing this would be our first and last date, I told him I hadn't brought my wallet, because I'd thought he was going to pay. In turn, he had the nerve to tell me I could pay him when he dropped me off. Can you believe he had the balls to say that?

My head starting spinning, imagining the scenario that was about to unfold: this guy was going to drive me back to my place in his Porsche and wait for me to go inside and come out and pay him for eating like a fucking pig.

The entire drive home, the fact that I had actually gone on a date with this douche-lord was making me more and more pissed off. By the time we got close to my apartment, I was really angry, at myself and him. But I remained pragmatic and devised a plan in my head.

When we got back to my place, he double-parked so that I could run up and get my wallet. I got out of his car. I went into my building, made sure the gate was tightly shut, and then went into my place. I locked my door, took off my clothes and got into my sweats, turned off all my lights, and gladly crawled into bed. There was no way in hell I was going to pay this asshole one single penny of my hard-earned money.

Oh, yes, he honked his horn once or twice, and my cell phone rang.

I turned my phone off.

I was not concerned that he would try to come up, nor did I care.

I heard his car screech away and soon after I fell asleep like a baby who just had its bottle.

Perhaps I should have just discussed dinner payment on our initial phone call like a hooker. Or perhaps I should send Vince a calculator?

Oh, by the way, did I ever tell you about the time I went to Saint Barts? What a douche.

**VINCE
AKA: EIGHTY-DOLLAR
CHICKEN SALAD**

CURTIS

I met Curtis at a gas station on Pico Boulevard in West Los Angeles. I realize that is an odd place to meet someone, but I don't believe in omens. It's possible to meet someone great anywhere. And it is just as easy to meet a complete asshole anywhere.

It was a Saturday afternoon and I was in the middle of running errands. It was a beautiful sunny day in Los Angeles, as it is 361 days of the year. We were both in workout clothes, so there wasn't much to hide when it came to our bodies. The candy was in the window and the shop doors were open, if you know what I mean.

He didn't ask my name, my age, where I lived, nor did he compliment me. He just handed me his card and said, "I gotta run." He was clearly too busy for me. *Refreshing*, I thought.

You see, people who are busy are so much sexier than "coffee shop chairs." What's a coffee shop chair? Anyone sitting at a coffee shop with flip-flops, jeans, and a T-shirt on a Monday at 2:00 p.m. In Los Angeles coffee shop chairs are most likely reading a script, writing a script, or thinking about a possible script. Big turnoff. I need someone with a job.

Anyway, having learned my lessons earlier in life regarding how fast to call someone back, I waited two days to call Curtis. I left him a voicemail (no one in LA answers their cell phones, even though they are attached to them like a wart) and I was poker-player cool in tone.

No intonations. No cracks in my voice. Calm. Collective. Masculine. "Hey, Curtis, we met at the gas station. I meant to call you yesterday but got sidetracked."

That was clearly a lie.

I continued, "If you get a chance, give me a call."

Interpretation: I am waiting for you because no one else is busy fucking me.

I hung up. One day went by. Two days went by. A week passed.

Now I started to think: *Did he get the message? Did my cell phone cut me off? But if he did get the message and I call again, I'm a stalker for sure.* And when you become a stalker, the word spreads fast—specifically in today's age of social media.

Eventually I thought, *If I don't call, I'll always wonder if he got the message.* So I called him again from my home phone to be sure the call went through. I spoke slowly, like in a time warp, and repeated my number twice.

In retrospect, it is quite possible my message made me sound like something is seriously wrong with me, and ironically, perhaps, I was the horrible one?

Curtis never called me back.

Curtis…I think I love you. I will pay for the entire wedding.

**CURTIS
AKA: GAS STATION LOVER**

▪◾ JC

I met JC at a bar in downtown Los Angeles. The bar was loud and crowded, but for some reason, I was extremely bored. I was leaving. My friends stayed behind, as is usually the case. JC was just arriving, and he grabbed me as I was walking out. He said, "You are too cute to be leaving."

He was right.

Not really, but his quick wit had my undivided attention. He was attractive enough to get away with his one-liner. Why is it that attractive people can get away with so much more?

We talked for only a few seconds and I was really leaving this time. I told him to look me up on Facebook.

If someone tells you to look them up, they are not that into you! I suggest you don't look them up.

I was not entirely into this guy, but his personality made him attractive. He was bold, and funny, and clearly he had his balls on the outside of his pants. Refreshing.

He looked me up the next day on Facebook and sent me a message with his phone number.

I figured, *Eh, why not?* So I called him and we spoke for a little while on the phone. Eventually I asked him what the initials JC stood for.

He paused and said, "Just call me JC."

There seemed to be an issue with his name or his willingness to share.

The first brick was in place for me to build a wall against him.

Over the course of several days, we had many more phone conversations. It took him weeks to tell me his real name. His real name is just too unique for me to say, and he would sue me if I even came close to using it. Just know it did not stand for Jesus Christ.

But what was worse than the initials-as-name debacle was the time we had sex. Yes, we had sex. Once. Sort of.

I went to his shit-hole apartment.

If you have nothing in life, just be really clean and it will make up for it.

We kissed a little. We got naked and began to have sex.

Oh wait, no we didn't.

He just laid there. He looked like a naked corpse with an erection.

He was lifeless.

I was tempted to check his pulse.

I had no idea what to do. I wasn't sure if he was expecting me to perform a *service* for him, like a masseuse does for married men on their way home from work.

So we "fooled around" a little. I think.

However, it was so dull and boring I began to wonder if perhaps he was touched by an angel. And then I started thinking more practical thoughts, like the fact that I was missing *American Idol* and that I had a lot of laundry to do.

We never had sex.

All I wanted was to do the dress-of-shame, do the walk-of-shame, and get the hell out of there.

So that's exactly what I did.

JC
AKA: NAKED AND LIFELESS

Danny

I met Danny through my friend Stacey. Getting introduced to someone through a friend is a great way to meet, but too often it doesn't seem to work out. You're not attracted to them. They're not attracted to you. You are smart, they are dumb, or vice versa. The odds of friends introducing you to your soul mate are very slim. It can happen, but I wouldn't rely on that.

We met at lunch, although it was not a fix-up. Danny and Stacey happened to be together one day when I called Stacey to see if she wanted to go to lunch. She had told me about Danny before, and I never thought he sounded like my type. When I finally met him, I thought he was very attractive. He had a scruffy face and good hair. He was tall and had a decent body. He wore great clothes, which made him seem more attractive. I'm always swayed by an attractive guy. Physical attraction is a *major* key element for men! I have met a lot of women who seem to be much more lenient about physical attraction being the most important factor in dating. Women are much more advanced on the evolutionary scale. I wish I were a lesbian. That seems like the perfect fit.

Still, I thought, *If Stacey likes him so much*, *then he must be a good guy*. So we exchanged phone numbers at lunch. I was willing to give it a shot, but at that moment it felt more like we would become just friends.

We went on a few dates, and I started to see that Danny was a great and solid guy. He had morals. He was caring. He loved his parents. He was from the Midwest. He had good values. He went to college. He made good money. He had good manners. He chewed with his mouth closed and did not lick his fingers. If someone licks their fingers at the dinner table, you have fun with that and good luck! He was the kind of guy everyone wants to be with or be like. Plus his sense of humor and fantastical talents in bed made up for any minor flaws.

Could he be for real? Not accustomed to someone so perfect, I began to look (literally) for things that could be wrong.

Here it comes.

I went through his drawers one morning, searching for something. I wanted to find that skeleton in the closet so he could seem more real. But nope, Danny was clean.

So I stopped looking. I thought, *Heck, why shouldn't I land a perfect guy? Why should I go looking for problems when there obviously were none?*

And that's when the problems found me.

About a month into dating, Danny and I were naked in bed after just having sex. He turned, looked at me, and he said, "I want kids."

Yes, with an "s."

Now, I know for some people this would be a dream. But I don't want kids. I don't even want *one*.

Someone once made me think I wanted kids. I know better now.

Still, though, Danny wanting kids wasn't the end per se; even if I don't want to raise kids, I appreciate that other people do. Then the other shoe dropped. Danny kept talking. He was going on and on, and I was still trying to wrap my head around what he had said. And then I heard him say that he thought one of us would have to quit working to raise the kids.

I looked over at him. He was giving me a look, clearly hinting it could be me who would stay at home. Apparently, he could visualize me as his own Mr. Mom.

Then it hit me: Danny didn't want a partner. He did not want a peer. He did not want an equal. He wanted a man-wife. I have no desire to live in a 1950s gay suburb.

His persona of good values, being a manly man, being the breadwinner wasn't something he was, it was something he was trying to move into. And all that was missing was the perfect man-wife to complete the Norman Rockwell picture. Except his version is an all-male, antiquated, paint by numbers. And apparently he had his eyes set on me as the protagonist.

Two gays and a baby, with me as the wife, no thank you. Sounds like a horrible sitcom.

We stayed in touch for a year or so and then our friendship faded away.

**DANNY
AKA: WANTS A MAN-WIFE**

◼◼ FRED

Although I know as little about medicine as most doctors seem to, I am fairly certain Fred might need to be on some type of medication.

It was the night of our first date, and Fred picked me up at my place in his car. Now, unlike some other cities, most dates in Los Angeles involve a car. If they didn't, it just wouldn't make any sense—sitting at a bus stop on a date is not romantic. Because of this, though, many people in LA judge others based on what kind of car they drive.

I've never been like that, as you now know. I couldn't care less what kind of car you drive. But that night I learned that I do care *how* my date drives, in that I would prefer not to get splattered across a highway.

Until I met Fred, I thought road rage was just another bullshit diagnosis to issue more drugs to our overmedicated society. Fred proved me wrong. Driving with Fred was like the running of the bulls— our car was the bull, and everyone else was simply running for their lives.

We drove to dinner at the speed of light as he bobbed and weaved his way through traffic like we were in a 3-D video game. He drove so fast we made every green light. It was the first and only time in my life I had driven anywhere in Los Angeles successfully making it through every green light. I have never in my life seen anyone drive like that.

I was terrified for my life.

Not only was Fred driving wildly, but he also honked at cars all along the way. If a car got in front of us *going the speed limit*, he would shout, "Fucking go, idiot!"

I was seriously frightened for my life. And by the time we got to dinner, I was not only frightened, I was nauseous.

You know how couples seem to find each other's

idiosyncrasies cute and adorable? How would I ever be able to find his driving cute? I wouldn't. Those are the same idiosyncrasies you end up hating about that person.

I don't even remember what happened at dinner, because by then, in my mind, it was over. All I wanted him to do was go home—in someone else's car—and throw up.

Finally, after another life-threatening ride back to my place, the date was over. But as we pulled up, another terrifying thought hit me: *What if he asks to come in?*

Luckily, at that time, my house was on a street that required parking permits. When we got back to my place I hopped out and said, "I would invite you in, but I don't have a permit." Clearly, he didn't have a permit either!

So, Fred, if I ever need to get to LAX during rush hour, I will call you. In the meantime, you may want to look into psychotherapy. This is a rare suggestion: please medicate.

Although it was a few years ago, my date with Fred was like being trapped in a modern, horrifying version of the video game *Frogger* at the most complicated level.

No one is safe when Fred is on the road.

FRED
AKA: ROAD RAGER

GARY

I met Gary while I was sitting at a coffee shop in Marina Del Rey. He came up to me (I *never* approach anyone), and we chatted for about fifteen minutes. He was a very successful real estate agent in Beverly Hills. He seemed to be very wealthy, overly man-scaped, and clean-cut. So when he asked me out, I said yes, even though I was not attracted to him and he seemed dull.

We decided to meet for our first date. Gary seemed like a decent guy. He was funny. He was better looking than before. We had a semi-decent first date.

We met for dinner in Westwood at a Chinese restaurant. Conversation was good and flowed well.

The bill arrived and he paid the entire bill with a credit card, stating that he could write it off as a business expense. That was a bit of a turnoff, but not a big deal.

Then we walked to get coffee, as I wanted to pay for something on the date so that there would be a sense of reciprocity. He got coffee and I got a hot tea. Afterward we walked and talked on the streets. We had some serious laughs. We had great conversation. We window-shopped at all the stores. We laughed about some of the window displays as we passed an "adult" store.

At the end of the night, we had a great long kiss good night and went our separate ways to our cars. It was like a corny montage from a corny date movie. By which I mean it was the perfect date.

I was in heaven. So I called him the next day and got his voicemail. I just said, "Hey, Gary, had a good time last night. Let me know when I can take you to dinner."

Weeks went by.

He never called again.

What the fuck?

To this day, I don't understand what happened. What seemed like the perfect date apparently was a horrible date for Gary. Maybe something happened after that night, like his uncle got hit by a car and was dragged seventeen blocks. I'll never know, though, and that's the horrible part.

I tried to mentally retrace my steps, my words, and my actions on that night. Did I do or say something horrible? Nope.

I promised myself if I ever saw Gary out, I would take the high road and say hi, all normal and unaffected. Two months later I got that opportunity when I saw him at a bar. But I didn't say a word. Why? I looked like shit that day.

Luckily, he didn't see me! I think.

**GARY
AKA: DID I MISS SOMETHING?**

:■ Mark

Mark was a vegan. As he explained, ad nauseam, being a vegan requires a much more serious commitment to food than being vegetarian. We went to a vegan restaurant for our date, and the food was totally bland. So was Mark.

As we "enjoyed" our date, he didn't ask much about me or tell me much about himself. No, instead I got a lecture about food and the human body. It was a super-sexy conversation.

Okay, of course it wasn't. Who wants to be lectured on a first date about how animals are treated and what meat does to the human body? GROSS! The date was a real flavor bomb that exploded and left shrapnel embedded in my body.

He rambled on and on about how humans should not eat meat.

And yet, as he proceeded to give me his lecture and to generally gross me out, I noticed something. He was wearing not one but several leather products.

He was wearing a leather belt and leather shoes.

So I asked him if he was wearing leather and he said, "Yes, what's your point?"

Now, as I leaned later in life, there are various types of vegans, some of whom do accept animal products on their bodies but do not eat animals. Confusing. I could now tell you all about the different types of vegans—but all of them are boring, so I won't waste your valuable time educating you on nonsense you want nothing to do with. If you don't eat meat, you shouldn't wear animals either.

It was just too confusing for me. I can, and do, respect vegans, I just don't want to date one. Vegans should really only date other vegans. Vegetarians, please fill out an application. Vegans need not apply! Meat eaters, call me for a date but don't make me dinner.

MARK
AKA: NIGHTMARE ON VEGAN STREET

JIM

I will spare you the details of how and where Jim and I met because our first date was ridiculous. All you need to know about Jim comes out in the one sentence he uttered to me on our first and final date. He wasted much more of my time than I am willing to waste of yours. I value you too much.

I arrived at his house for our first date after being excited all day. I approached his dumpy unkempt house and knocked on the door. I suppose the condition of the exterior of his house should have given me some type of warning, but as I said, I was excited.

I knocked on the door.

Instead of the knob turning and my date greeting

me warmly with a hug and a kiss, I heard a shout: "Come in."

Strike one. He had already lost major points for not coming to the door to greet me.

I opened the door and there he was in all his amazing glory. He was sitting on his couch in sweatpants and a wife-beater tank top. Strike two.

His house was a wreck. Strike three. There were pizza boxes piled up on the coffee table. Empty beer cans were squished on the floor, on the couch, and all over the place. His house was dark and scary—like what I thought a serial killer's home might look like. I started looking around to see if he had ropes and tape nearby or a well in the center of the room. He didn't.

Not spotting any instruments of my impending murder, I sat down on the couch next to him and said, "Do you need me to give you time to get ready?" I was hoping he would get the clue that he looked like hell and I was not going out with him looking like that.

Deep down I was convinced he just wasn't ready and that he was going to jump in the shower and clean up. Regardless, the condition of this house was unforgettable and truly frightening. I was seriously scared and I wanted to get the hell out of there.

He looked right at me, with a stone-cold-serious face, and said:

"Are you cool with stayin' in, ordering Chinese food, and getting high?"

I didn't say a single word. I turned around and left.

Instead of slamming the door like a drama queen, I left it open so that his gross, filthy, lazy ass would have to get up and close it himself.

I walked to my car, got in, locked the doors, and called my friend Sabrina from my cell phone to see if she was free to go out, and she met me out for dinner.

NOT Chinese food!

**JIM
AKA: WEED AND
CHINESE FOOD**

CRAIG

A little over a year after the infamous 1994 Northridge earthquake in Los Angeles, it seemed as though folks here were getting back to their daily grind. Once the dust settled from that tragic morning, Angelenos seemed more courteous and sincere. That didn't last very long. By the end of 1995 the majority of assholes here had gotten right back into their game. I, on the other hand, was left with glimpses of hope that people had changed. What I didn't realize is that when you shake off the dust from a lemon, it's still a lemon—sour.

One very early morning in December, I knew the forecast was to be sunny and warm. No shock there, but anticipating the joy of a warm day in December, I decided I would pull myself together at 7:00 a.m. and go to Venice Beach to go bike riding or rollerblading. Being able to bike ride or rollerblade up and down California's coast is unlike any experience anywhere. It is surreal. Beautiful people in almost no clothing, beautiful weather, panoramic views, sailboats on the water's horizon—Los Angeles really is heaven on earth (unless you start talking to people who live here).

I decided to rent rollerblades that day. If I had rented a bike, I would never have met Craig. Looking back, the bike would have been the better choice.

I was rollerblading down the cement path, enjoying the views and glory created by mother nature. The sight was about to improve drastically.

A ridiculously *hot* guy rollerbladed right up behind me. Letting me know he was going to pass me to my left, he yelled, "On your left." As he passed, he looked at me, which is when I noticed how fucking gorgeous he was. He looked at me again, and I yelled out, "On your right." He looked back, yelled, "Good one," smiled, and kept rollerblading.

When he rollerbladed away, I visualized him in a tux slipping a ring on my finger. All I could think about was how good we would look together when we went walking down the marriage aisle. I would love him permanently just based on his looks. He was six foot two with a thirty-two-inch waist, the arms of a Trojan warrior, crystal-clear skin, and amazing thick black hair with just a few strands of gray. He had a bubble butt that you could set this book on and read it for hours. He was wearing sunglasses. When his sunglasses came off, I saw that he had green-brown-yellow-flecked eyes.

He was way out of my league. In fact, I wasn't on the same field, or even in the same sport. If we did get married, I would always wake up being the ugly one. But that's okay—his good looks would escalate my looks, putting me into a new category. I was prepared for my new role as *hot*. Unfortunately, he kept rollerblading, leaving me to think he was not interested. Or even worse—he was straight.

As he rolled out of view, he took my heart with

him. How were we going to become a rollerblading pairs' championship team and travel the world signing autographs when I didn't even know who he was?

Eventually I said to myself, *Okay, he was gay, but he must just be in a relationship*. So I let it go.

Ironically, as soon as you let something go, it seems to come back to you full force.

As the thought of my rollerblading dream man was vanishing, I decided to blade up to a concession stand. And who do you think was right in front of me? Yep, it was him. His bubble butt was staring me in the face. By that I mean, my face was staring at his butt.

I suddenly became nervous. He didn't know I was behind him. Should I say something funny? Would it actually be funny? Should I cough? Should I grab his ass? Should I pretend to trip into him even though I am a really good skater? Should I just stand behind him like a dumb-ass, hoping he will see me?

I thought, *Okay, if there is a God, now he will give my rollerblading lover a reason to turn around*. He didn't turn around. God, where were you that day? Were you busy only hooking up straight people? That's rude.

Suddenly, I decided I would be proactive and say something. I shouted, "On your back." I was horrified—I had meant to say, "On your right."

He turned around and said, "On my back, already?"

Oh my god, I thought, *not only is this guy fucking gorgeous, but he has a sense of humor too*. JACKPOT, VEGAS, WINNING, MARRIAGE…

He said, "Hi, I'm Craig, what's your name?" and reached out his hand to shake hello. I reached out my hand and mentally slipped on the wedding ring. I was imagining him asking me to move in and rent movies every night and ignore the world.

We both bought bottled water, and he asked if I wanted to sit and talk. I was going to order a soda and nachos, but his bottled water order put me under pressure.

Of course I wanted to sit with him. I wanted to sit on his face, sit on his lap, sit on his bed, sit on his couch, sit on anything he wanted me to sit on. I was not being myself. Suddenly, I was a little girly, inse-cure mess. But instead of showing my insecurity and insanity, I built a brick wall around myself and only showed Craig my sense of humor. I thought, *At least he'll find me funny.*

We talked for about an hour. The conversation was great. He was polite, funny, and so attractive. The more he spoke, the brighter the glow that I visualized around him intensified. If a mom could go shopping for her son's or daughter's husband or wife, she would shop for Craig.

Take a moment to take that last sentence in and interchange the variables.

As it turned out, Craig was gay and he was single. We exchanged phone numbers, and the rest of my day was the best rollerblading experience of my life.

But it was all about to come crashing down. Because something Craig did not share with me at the beach (nor should he have) popped up on our first, and only, date.

I called Craig the next day and left him a voicemail

just to say, "Great meeting you." Which it was. I just wanted to be in contact and be sincere regardless of the outcome.

He called me back within an hour. We spoke on the phone, and we seemed to have a lot in common. He liked hiking, rollerblading, and being outside. He was close to his family and had a really close bond with his sister. These were all things I completely identified with.

This is the point where you start to analyze and imagine scenarios of why someone like Craig is still single. He had said he didn't go to bars. He hardly ever went out. He'd had a long-term relationship that had broken up two years earlier, but they had remained good friends. My standard get-to-know someone checklist seemed intact, and Craig came across as a near-perfect guy. I wondered yet again, *What the fuck is he doing single?* Then it dawned on me like a glorious religious epiphany. The rays of sunlight were shining through the cloudy sky. I realized he was single because he was meant to be with me (the uglier one compared to him) so he could wake up gorgeous for the rest of his life.

Count me in for the long haul.

No such luck. At the end of our first date I knew why he was single—or at least why it would "take a village" to date him.

For our first date I drove to pick up Craig. We went to dinner at a very nice restaurant on La Cienega Boulevard. I didn't have any drinks, so bear in mind that I was completely sober for the entire date. A rare occurrence.

Conversation was really good. Craig was only paying attention to me and not everyone else in the place. He was really into me, and I was *really* into him. I could find *nothing* wrong with this dude. *Why? This just can't be as good as it seems.*

Soon I realized that it wasn't as good as it seemed. Craig proceeded to get really, really drunk. He was not a belligerent or loud drunk; it was probably obvious only to me, and the waiter, that Craig had way too much to drink.

As Craig ordered drink after drink during dinner, I didn't want to say anything. Who wants to be on a first date with some douche who starts saying, "Don't you think you have had enough?" No one wants to be out with that person. Besides, Craig wasn't driving and he'd had a hard week at work. He worked in mortgage loans, and in 1995 the government was at the height of giving millions of dollars to people to buy homes when those people only made thirty thousand dollars a year, so he worked really long hours, ten to twelve hours a day.

Finally, though, he broke his glass when he knocked it against his plate. At that point the waiter cut him off. We left soon after, much to my relief.

A buzzed date can be charming on a first date. A really drunk first date is a bit less charming.

On the car ride home, Craig started to ask sexual questions. But from the perspective of a drunk—no boundaries, no limits, no social filter.

He said, "Do you have a huge penis?" I ignored the question. My penis is a great size, but I didn't want to encourage the conversation. I thought it best to just let him enjoy himself, but not partake in drunk sex talk since I was sober. That didn't stop him. The rest of the drive home took about twenty minutes, and the entire ride consisted of Craig telling me over and over that his penis is "HUGE" and that everyone freaks out when they see his dick.

After twenty minutes of belligerent big dick talk, I was finally sort of fascinated and interested. I thought, *He's probably one of those guys with a small dick and has convinced himself that it's huge.* My guess is that one out of two guys has a misconstrued idea of his own dick size.

When we got to Craig's apartment building, I pulled over. I put on my hazard lights and put the car in park. I'd had enough of Craig's boasting, and knowing he was really drunk I figured I had nothing to lose. So I said, "Pull out your dick."

At which point, Craig pulled out his dick.

And I was like, *What the fuck, are you kidding me?*

Craig's penis was not huge.

It was monumental, in a *Guinness-Book-of-Records-*type category.

However, this was not a good thing. Craig had a medical condition known as elephantiasis of the penis. His penis looked like it was allergic to shellfish and had just eaten a plate full. It was about ten inches around, ten inches in length, and his balls were about the same.

My eyes went wide.

I was horrified. It was the ugliest penis I have ever seen in my life. It looked like a two-pound water balloon with ten pounds of water inside it. His penis was distorted and bubbled up in certain spots. It looked like it had swallowed five penises and hadn't finished digesting them.

With this vision clouding my mind, I was speechless. Unfortunately, super-drunk Craig was not speechless. He grabbed his monster penis and said to me, "Look at this, I can't wait to stretch you out."

I felt like I was in a terrible porn that tried to incorporate a story line.

Finally I was able to talk.

I looked him in the eye and said, "I won't ever be able to do anything with that."

I could see he paused in thought and hesitated before putting the beast back in its cage.

He zipped up, got out of the car, and went into his building. I did not drive away abruptly; I sat there for a few minutes and just laughed at myself. I realized that my decade-long focus on finding a guy with an above average penis had produced elephant-size results.

The next day he probably waited for me to call. I spent the day hoping *he* would never call. Days and weeks went by, and neither of us contacted the other. I was in the clear.

His looks may have been out of my league, but I could never compete with that penis, nor was there any way I could entertain it. We were not a good match—I would always lose.

CRAIG
AKA: ELEPHA-
ANAPHYLACTIC SHOCK

▪■ PAUL

Paul thought he was so funny. I did not. I care too much about you, my reader, to have you know anything more about Paul other than the essentials, and that can be summed up in a few words.

He told jokes all the time. He took nothing seriously. While that sounds like it could be nice and refreshing, believe me, it's not. It's spooky.

We were on our first date, enjoying a nice dinner. Trying to get to know him better, I asked if he had siblings.

He said, "Yes, one brother..." He then paused for a few seconds, and said, "Who I used to fuck when we were little."

I was dumbfounded.

I sat there silent with my jaw open.

He sat there with a stupid self-pleased grin, waiting for me to react. Then a few minutes later he said, "Just kidding!"

Yeah. By then it was too late.

He could tell, though, from my lack of laughter and my body language, that I didn't think his joke was funny.

And, as a last desperate measure for a humorous reaction from me, he asked, "Would it bother you if I had fucked him?"

I was stone faced. Not a muscle moved. I did not even blink—on purpose.

I will spare you any more jokes from Paul. Just like his jokes, nothing about the rest of the night was funny!

If Paul really has a brother, I feel sorry for him.

**PAUL
AKA: FUCKS HIS BROTHER**

WILLIAM

William was good in bed, but he liked sports as much as he liked himself. That would put me in third place—forever.

Don't get me wrong, I love sports. I'm very competitive. I will watch almost any sport except baseball and women's basketball (boring).

William's love of sports wasn't necessarily a problem. What was a problem was what happened after two "just okay" dates.

I guess they were good enough, since after the second date we both got naked. But after fooling around for a while in the dark, suddenly he wasn't there.

As I was trying to figure out where the fuck he had gone, suddenly William popped out of his closet.

He was wearing his hockey mask and said, "I am an intruder…rape me for breaking into your home… punish this intruder…"

I wasn't sure if it was a joke or if he seriously wanted to do this weird role-play. My instincts told me he was serious, but he would pass it off as a joke if I didn't like what he was doing. I was not about to find out either way. While this may have been tongue-in-cheek for William, it was really stupid and a huge turnoff.

William in a hockey mask immediately made me think of Jason from *Friday the 13th*, and who's going to be able to have sex while being worried about getting slashed? I didn't want to wind up in a jar of formaldehyde on his shelf, so I pretended I had developed an immediate bout of food poisoning, and I got dressed and left.

The glory of always going to someone else's house on a date is that you control when the date is over.

This date was over and there would not be another.

Still, as karma would have it, I actually did come down with food poisoning the following day and ended up at the hospital several days later from dehydration. Now that is karma!

**WILLIAM
AKA: FRIDAY THE 13TH**

▗▄ SERGIO

I went on a vacation to Tijuana, Mexico. It was the summer of 2000, and I was in a new-millennium kind of good mood. Y2K? Whatever! What a crock of shit that was.

So that summer when my good friend Brian suggested we head off to Mexico for my birthday, I was in. We were ready for sun, swimming, chips and salsa, and margaritas for a week. We both just really wanted to get out of Los Angeles—away from the smog, the traffic, and the total assholes who live here. (Ironically, the only way to truly tolerate Los Angeles is to travel out of LA to places where people are human and nice. Then you come back and realize that LA has the best weather on the planet.)

Now, neither of us had gone to Mexico intending to get laid or meet someone. I know enough to know that if you travel to get laid, it's likely to happen only when you don't want it. Hunting for sex is a doomed quest. Give it up Indiana Boner, it won't happen that way.

So we went to Mexico just to have fun. We were staying at a hotel that Brian informed me was right next to a new hot-spot gay bar.

We had no intention of going to bars, but once Brian divulged our convenient proximity to a bar, somehow I knew we would end up there.

And yes, on our first night there we grabbed a quick bite in the hotel restaurant…and then we were off to the bar we had said we wouldn't go to.

Within ten minutes of being at the bar, two really sexy Latin guys were all over us. Neither of them spoke English well, but they spoke it enough to make sense. Sort of.

They may have just liked us to score green cards, but that would have been okay.

We'd had some drinks with dinner and were already a little buzzed. We danced, had drinks, laughed, and quickly became quite toasted.

We closed the bar down and then all went to get some food. We were really drunk and walked to some trashy diner that was most likely cooking alley cats and dogs. We ordered all kinds of food and acted like drunk asses to the waitress. Typical vacation fun.

We were one drink shy of drunk karaoke on vacay.

The guy I liked was named Sergio. He was tall, with a great body and that super-smooth, hairless Latin skin that looks like silky chocolate milk. He was fun, smart, wild, sexy, and had a great energy to him. I was so into him.

He told me he was moving to Studio City, California, with his friend in a few months, so I began imagining that he could be my future lover. Suddenly I didn't want to just hook up with him, I wanted to date him. So I didn't invite him to my hotel—instead we exchanged numbers and made plans for a date the following night. I was really feeling proud of myself for resisting the hookup, and stayed focused on the potential for future long-term bliss.

And then…

He insisted he just wanted to come back to my hotel to kiss and cuddle—no sex!

Hot Latin men can be so persuasive. Kissing and cuddling sounded great.

Sergio came back to my hotel. And yes, within five minutes of being there we were completely naked, crashing through the room, ripping off each other's clothes like two piranhas fighting in a glass jar.

He then sat me on the edge of the bed. He got on his knees and started to "service" me (his words).

But that didn't last long.

Sergio tried to get creative by shoving my penis all the way down his throat, which isn't an easy task. Unfortunately, whether it was the drinks or the gag reflex, it didn't work out quite like Sergio, or I, expected.

He threw up all over me.

This wasn't just any kind of throw up. It was violent, like something from *The Exorcist*, full of colors that to this day I have yet to see on a color wheel. I was waiting for his head to start spinning around.

And then…Well…I have an extremely sensitive stomach. So the sight and smell of Sergio's vomit all over my naked body caused me to throw up all over him.

I wish I were making this up, but I'm not.

I jumped up and ran to the shower to clean myself off. Sergio followed me into the shower to do the same.

When we got out of the shower, I told him I had to get up early, so he should go and I would call him tomorrow. I didn't. Ironically, just a few hours earlier I had been imagining we would be together forever. Stupefying how quickly we can change our minds about something.

I wonder if he ever moved to Studio City.

Now, any time anyone mentions Mexico, I think of vomit.

**SERGIO
AKA: MEXICO**

MIKE

Driving home from Laguna Beach one Saturday afternoon, I went to a bar in Long Beach that I had been to before. It was a really cool hangout where there was no attitude. It was like a gay Cheers, but on the coast, and gay. So really, it wasn't much like Cheers at all.

It was a really hot day. I was in shorts and flip-flops, and I looked like hell, but I didn't care. I just wanted to stop in and have a drink and hang out for a while. The last thing on my mind was meeting someone.

In fact, I was hoping I would be ignored.

I was sitting at the bar when a semi-cute guy approached me. When you're single, and a semi-cute person is trying to get your attention, you are often on the fence about reciprocating.

There is a term in dating nicknamed "G.U." Translation: Geographically Undesirable. In Los Angeles, anyone who lives farther than ten miles away from you is G.U., because any time of day or night, besides 3:00 a.m., it will take you two hours to get there in a car.

I'm not normally a stickler for the G.U. concept. But as I said, he was semi-cute and I looked like shit, so I had better play my cards correctly.

I asked him where he lived and some other general questions.

He was nice and everything seemed okay.

However, Mike lived in North Carolina. What a bummer that information was.

Are you kidding me? Why would I, or you, want to start dating someone who lives across the country?

If this was the gay Cheers, this guy was not my Woody.

Long distance rarely works and it is way too much effort for me.

Save yourself a lot of time and money and try to date locals only.

**MIKE
AKA: FLIGHT CANCELLED**

SOMeGUY

We made eye contact for way too long while both sitting in our cars at a red light at Santa Monica Boulevard and Doheny Drive. It was the middle of the day—a Wednesday, I think. The light turned green. We both took off slowly, trying to get each other's attention. I could feel his eyes on me. I looked over and I was right.

I thought, *Will he get away? Can I drive any slower without getting a ticket?* So many thoughts rushed through my head. Could he be THE ONE?

Finally, at the next red light, he motioned for me to pull over. So I did.

I got out of my car and walked around to the passenger side of Someguy's car. I was about to start a conversation, but through his rolled-down passenger window I could see that Someguy was nude from the waist down. Except for a pair of black lace women's panties and high heels.

I stepped back and said, "Dude, what the hell are you wearing?"

He said, "I am a lady and I need a man."

I was speechless.

I turned around and walked back to my car. I got in, sat down, closed the door, locked both doors, and busted up in laughter. The type of hard-core laughter that causes tears and a little pee.

Minutes later, the analytical side of me thought, *How the hell did he learn to drive in pumps?*

**SOMEGUY
AKA: THE LADY**

DAVID

I was set up on a blind date with David by my really good friend Liora. I had confidence that Liora could find a match for me. I trusted Liora and her judgment with everything. She was my high school best friend and we had been friends for over a decade. She had great taste. She was drop-dead gorgeous; every man turned his head when she walked by. She looked like a dark-haired Katherine Heigl. She was one of the most beautiful, and smartest, people I knew.

Liora and I had very similar ideas about whom we thought to be attractive, so I knew I could fully trust her judgment. For months she told me about this guy she thought was perfect for me. She said he was tall, dark-haired, nice, funny, creative, and about to graduate with a PhD. He sounded great, but for some odd reason I continually brushed it off.

After nearly six months of being reminded by Liora that she had the perfect date for me, I gave in. I told Liora to give this guy my number.

David called me. We spoke on the phone for about an hour, maybe more. We mostly spoke about Liora, since that was our only common ground. She was easy to speak about, because she was so amazing. David mentioned that Saturday nights were better for him because he was usually so tired on Friday nights from work. That made perfectly good sense. I like people who make sense, which is why I don't like most people.

David and I spoke again on Saturday afternoon before our date. We had a good conversation, and he shared a little more about himself, his hobbies, what he liked to do in his spare time. Everything seemed fine. There was only one thing that struck me as unusual. He mentioned that he liked magicians and magic.

We all like a certain element of magic in our lives,

but he was the first person I ever met who claimed to like actual magic.

Imagine you are a grade-school kid kissing someone for the first time at the school carnival. You are on the Ferris wheel as it rounds the top. No one can see you, there is a view, there is a slight chill in the air. You put your arm around her or him for the first time. You are nervous. It is exciting. It is special. You have your first kiss. The kiss is unlike anything you could have imagined. You will remember that kiss for the rest of your life, as if it were magical.

Now get that image out of your head.

That's not the type of magic David will be associated with.

Saturday night, at 7:00 p.m. on the dot, my doorbell rang. I opened the door to a tall, dark-haired guy who seemed quite attractive. However, I noticed he was crossing one of his eyes. I invited him in and I started to laugh. I closed the door, still laughing, and I said to him through my laughter, "I get it…a cross-eyed blind date. That is fucking hilarious." I then said, "You have a great sense of humor, I like that."

David said, "Didn't Liora mention I have a crossed eye?"

I thought it was still part of the joke, so I said, "Okay, funny, I get it, joke's on me."

David then became serious and said, "I'm not kidding, nor am I doing this as a joke. I was born with a crossed eye and people always think it's a joke."

At this point, reality struck...David had one crossed eye and not two crossed eyes. I was mortified at myself. I began to sweat.

I didn't know what to do except apologize, so I did. He said, "No problem, it's not the first time."

I realized that the only way I could handle the rest of this date, and forgive my own ignorance, was to get really drunk. I knew that if I stayed sober I would only talk to his good eye, not the one making the permanent left turn, and it would be really obvious. So I offered to make us drinks.

My place had an open bar area that faced the

kitchen. So I motioned for David to come over to the bar.

David was attractive, but I was not prepared for the crossed eye thing. Liora had never mentioned this. I suddenly realized why. She never said anything bad about anyone. She didn't want me to judge him before our date, which I would have. She had her heart in the right place on that, but I must say it backfired.

I needed mental preparation for this date.

I needed the pertinent information before our date. Not mentioning someone is cross-eyed for a blind date is a significant omission.

This was not only a blind date, it was pre-Facebook, pre-social media. David and I walked into the kitchen, and he sat at the bar as I got out glasses and pulled my vodka from the freezer. A good drunk keeps vodka in the freezer. My back was turned to him as I made the drinks, and when I turned around the date got worse.

In the midst of me making us drinks, I turned around and David had whipped out a deck of cards from his pocket. He said, "Let me show you some magic tricks I learned from David Copperfield."

He began flipping cards and asked me to think of a number. All I could come up with in my mind was, "Get out."

That was six letters, so I said, "Six."

He pulled out a six.

I was wondering if he was going to whip out a balloon and make animal figures. That I would have liked!

This was *way* too much for me to handle. Here was a guy on our blind date who was cross-eyed and then began doing magic tricks. *Are you fucking kidding me?*

Now, to be clear, David was probably a great guy. But I have no idea, because when we went to dinner, all I could think about was his magic tricks and *which* eye I should speak to. David's first impression didn't just leave a memory. It left a skid mark, a dent, and a scar.

He was really nice, and I am sure someone snatched him up. I just know my own limits and this was for sure one, two, of them.

I called Liora the next morning and asked her why she hadn't told me about the eye and the use of magic. She said. "Because you would have judged him before meeting him."

She was right.

She did explain, though, that she had known David liked magic tricks but had no clue he would show up trying his material.

She laughed, I laughed.

Regardless of the events, David and I had nothing in common. We never went out again. Every time I think about our date, it makes me laugh. David, I should probably thank you for years of laughter. Where are you anyway? Did you *disappear*? Perhaps you were a better magician than I realized.

**DAVID
AKA: THE CROSS-EYED
MAGICIAN**

▄▟ CLIFF-NOTeS

A psychologist I know heard that I was writing this book. No, I don't go to a shrink. If I did go to a shrink, I would admit it. If I do in the future, I will admit it because there is nothing wrong with therapy. But this psychologist is really just a friend.

He said I should make sure some of the stories in the book were really brief so that the reader would get a great sense of accomplishment from a super-short story. "Maybe your reader is on the go, or only has a few minutes to read a quick story. Maybe he or she's even waiting for a date to pick him or her up." I told him I didn't want to trick my readers and this book was entirely truthful.

I told him I had several date stories that were

quite short, some of them only a couple of sentences. He said, *perfect*.

CLIFF

I met Cliff at a computer class for Adobe Illustrator. The class was in West Hollywood, which is one of the gay meccas of the planet (next to San Francisco). So odds were, I figured, someone other than me in the class would be gay.

BINGO.

Cliff was already at an advanced Illustrator level, so he was taking the course just as a refresher. Maybe he was there to boost his ego. I was a beginning student— almost a virgin. I decided that I needed him.

We hit it off and were flirting a bit, and eventually he asked me out on a date. If he hadn't asked me I would have asked him. So the interest level was mutual.

What I *did not* need was Cliff crying on our first date.

On our date Cliff began to share information about his ex-partner. Cliff broke down crying while describing how he came home to find his lover cheating on him, in their bed (that he paid for) with his best friend.

This was indeed a sad story.

However, watching a man cry on a first date was super awkward. Everyone in the restaurant looked at us like I was breaking up with him. Some people even gave me a dirty look.

It was all just too much for me to handle. Class dismissed.

CLIFF
AKA: NO MORE TEARS

TROY

Do you remember my date with Ben? I'm pretty sure Troy was up to the exact same thing as Ben—licking toilets. Perhaps I should fix them up.

> **TROY**
> **AKA: HALI-TROY-SIS**

JEFF

I met Jeff outside a Mexican restaurant in the San Fernando Valley while we were both waiting for our cars to be brought around by the valet. Jeff said, "I like your jeans, where did you get them?" Not original but good enough to get me to talk. I should have known then. Still, we chatted for a few seconds and he suggested we exchanged numbers. So we did.

We had just one phone conversation. That nearly put me to sleep.

Our conversation had silent moments that seemed to last an eternity. He was the most boring person I have ever met. He was causing me to yawn into the phone. He asked if I was tired and I said yes even though I wasn't before he called. Trying to get Jeff to talk was like watching a dead tree grow new leaves. He was so boring. Boring might be a worse quality than being dumb.

However, I should thank Jeff for the incredible night of sleep I got. I wish I could give you all his number, for if you ever have insomnia. Insomnia is really fucking annoying.

> **JEFF**
> **AKA: THE SLEEPING PILL**

FRANKIE

I met Frankie at Nordstrom at The Grove, while I was diligently shopping for a new pair of jeans. Why is it so fucking difficult to find the perfect pairs of jeans? He was staring at me and eventually came up and said hello. We talked for a few minutes. He asked me if I was single, and we chatted a while. We exchanged phone numbers.

We talked on the phone that week about three times before deciding to go on our first date. In all of our calls, Frankie seemed smart and nice.

Apparently, though, he's *not* very smart.

On our first date, things were going well. Until Frankie said he had to step outside the restaurant to smoke a cigarette.

Anyone who smokes cigarettes is not for me. It never dawned on me to ask him if he smoked, because I assume anyone with a fifth-grade education is smart enough *not* to smoke cigarettes. Unless you live in the backwoods of Timbuktu, are missing the majority of your teeth, and your parents are brother and sister, you should be smart enough to know that tobacco causes cancer, which leads to death. Yes, that was a run-on sentence. Settle down.

It never dawned on me to ask someone before a first date if he smoked. Now I always ask that question. Smoking cigarettes is a deal breaker for me.

For those of you reading this who smoke, please stop smoking. My uncle died of lung cancer, and I wish he were still here. I'm not trying to preach. I just care about all of my readers and want you to live. If this rant gets one person to quit smoking, I will be happy.

FRANKIE
AKA: CIGARETTE BREAK

JONN

I met Jonn while getting frozen yogurt at a very popular yogurt shop in Los Angeles. You won't need the details in between, because our first and only dinner date was filled with information that I don't think anyone would want to know on a first date, or ever.

He told me that he had changed the spelling of his name from John to Jonn because he felt too ordinary with the common spelling. He told me to make sure I spell his name right.

That already annoyed me.

At first I didn't think too much of that, but I quickly learned that his name spelling was a sign of a person with a mammoth mountain of issues. He had his own personal landfill of drama and baggage.

Over the course of the dinner, he told me that:

- He hated his mom. "She's a bitch."

- He doesn't speak to anyone in his family.

- His uncle molested him for ten years.

Now, don't get me wrong. I am very empathetic towards bad childhoods, and I would never judge someone for that. I could be the poster child for fucked-up childhoods, but the timing of the information dump was disturbing, to say the least. If someone is willing to divulge everything from his past to you on a first date, take it as a sign saying, *Run, don't walk!*

> **JONN**
> **AKA: SPELLING BEE**

ROBIN

Yes, a man named Robin. Since this is his real name, I can't tell you our story. But I'm guessing he had a childhood that was complicated and involved a lot of hiding during lunch breaks. A man named Robin might fare well in England and not get beat up at recess, but in the United States he is fair game and can expect routine beatings and taunts.

I am not promoting teasing, bullying, or fights. I am simply stating that a boy named Robin in the USA won't have an easy childhood. I am not even going to acknowledge Batman jokes...

It wasn't just his name, though. Ever go on a

dinner date and the food was better than the date? He was just boring.

I may have given him another shot, but the name tipped the decision toward a no. It's funny how you can be on the fence about liking someone and something as simple as their name, or something they are wearing, can spoil the whole thing. Unless he was robbing from the rich and giving to the poor I did not want to see his forest. That would have made him interesting.

ROBIN
AKA: ROBIN HOOD

:■ TONY

S ocial media has changed everything from dating, to business communication, to electing a president. We are just not the same society as we were before so much online/electronic nonsense and the absence of real one-on-one communication. I think soon there will be a "Social Media Disorder" that requires pills for treatment. I can hear someone saying it at a party: "I have SMD."

But what does social media have to do with a date that took place in 1997? We shall see.

In July 1997, on a Saturday night, my friend Dawnne and I went to a landmark gay bar in Studio City called Oil Can Harry's. Oil Can's housed everything from leather daddies and young twinks, to old perverts and jocks. However, Oil Can's was known mostly for its country-western scene.

Imagine this: Los Angeles, palm trees, yuppies, and two gay country-western guys in ten-gallon hats, tight jeans, and boots, holding hands walking down Ventura Boulevard. It doesn't get any better than that.

Dawnne and I were dancing, drinking, and having a great time. The disco ball was spinning and the strobe lights were darting through the club like a laser show.

Old queens were up on stage with tambourines, tight jeans, and no shirts. It was fucking brilliant.

We were enjoying the surprise of it being retro seventies night at Oil Can's. Just when you thought Oil Can's wasn't confused enough, you learn that, yes, they had a disco night. Oil Can's was like a box of chocolates—who knows what the fuck is inside, but you will probably eat the entire box anyway.

An average-looking guy came up to Dawnne and started talking to her. I thought, *This sucks, I take a girl to a gay bar and she meets someone in thirty minutes or less.*

I was wrong, though.

His name was Tony, and he had approached Dawnne to ask her if I was her boyfriend because he thought I was cute. When I found this out an hour later, I thought Tony was charming and his shyness was attractive. Normally, I would have found that sophomoric and a turnoff.

I think if everyone walked around a little bit buzzed we would all be a lot nicer to each other.

Tony danced with us, bought us both drinks, and we all got plastered. We closed that place down. Then we walked to the famous Du-par's Restaurant on Laurel and Ventura. It was 2:30 a.m. by this point. We were drunk and belligerent. We ate a table load of greasy food, and it is a sin to exit Du-Pars without eating pie. So, we ate an entire pie.

I didn't talk much to Tony, because I was really drunk and I didn't care that much about him just yet. I also had forgotten his name and was too embarrassed to ask him again.

We left the diner at about 3:30 a.m. Tony and I

exchanged numbers (actual landline telephone numbers), and the three of us went our separate ways. Dawnne came home with me for a drunk slumber party. Those are the best.

Four days later, at which point I had already forgotten about him, Tony called. I was young then and really self-involved, like most young people. We spoke briefly. We discussed our ages, where we were born, and just some basics. He asked if I wanted to go out again to Oil Can's to dance. I thought that would be perfect. I was not sure I liked him, so if I didn't I could spend the night looking for someone else and burn calories dancing. It was a date, but had no pressure of good conversation—perfect.

Tony picked me up at 10:00 p.m. and we dashed off to Oil Can Harry's. When we got there, the place was nearly empty. So we just sat at one of the two bars and Tony ordered vodka. I ordered 7-Up. For some odd reason, my instincts told me not to drink. I was worried that I might get really drunk and let Tony into my bed later.

It was odd that I listened to my instincts. How many times have you not listened to your instincts? You do something you know you shouldn't, it goes wrong, and then you blame yourself. I do that all the time, but not that night.

As the night marched on, Tony ordered more and more vodkas, and I continued to drink 7-Up. (Tip: if you're not drinking, holding a glass of 7-Up with a lime wedge makes you look like you're drinking alcohol and not some douche drinking water in a bar.)

At about 11:30 p.m., I began to realize that Tony was my only ride home, and that we'd better get out of there before he got too wasted to drive. So I said, "Let's go back to my place and get naked."

I had no intention of getting naked, but I knew that a drunk *never* wants to leave a bar early unless he has a good reason. By this point, Tony had had four drinks in the previous hour and had just downed two more drinks. I wanted to get us home before the last two drinks kicked in.

That didn't happen.

We got into Tony's car and headed east down Ventura Boulevard toward Toluca Lake. Within four blocks of the bar, police lights started flashing behind us. As Tony pulled over, I said, "Act calm and don't breathe in his direction. Do NOT freak out." I then quickly said, "Are all your insurance papers and shit in the glove compartment?"

Tony froze and didn't say a word. Before Tony could find his voice, an officer shined a light in his eyes and said, "Step out of the car."

What neither of us knew then, but I found out a few months later, was that the cops hid on side streets off Ventura Boulevard and waited for guys to come out of the gay bars, drunk and driving, then pull them over.

The officer asked Tony to step onto the sidewalk to perform some sobriety tests. He tried walking a line and he could not. He tried to touch his nose but touched his mouth. He breathed into a mouthpiece. He failed all of the tests. The officer then handcuffed Tony and put him in the back of his car. The officer then came up to me on the passenger side of the car and asked me to roll down the window.

"Have you been drinking also?" he asked.

"No, I have not had one drink, and I can pass every single test you just gave him."

The officer stared into my eyes for a good solid minute, and then he said, "Wait here." He walked back to the police car.

I was trying to look in the rearview mirror to see what was going on. But it wasn't positioned for the passenger. I was reaching up to angle the mirror toward the police car when I heard on a bullhorn:

"DON'T MOVE OR I WILL SHOOT YOU."

I nearly shit my pants. I froze dead in my tracks.

I forgot that the entire car was under a police car spotlight. Needless to say, I didn't move a muscle after that.

Twenty minutes later the police officer came up to my window again.

"Can you drive this car home?"

I said, "Are you kidding me?"

He said, "Do I act like I'm kidding? Your friend here is about to get a DUI, and the bad part is that he's on probation from a DUI he got seven months ago." The officer explained that he could impound the vehicle, but he didn't want to leave me stranded.

I explained to the officer that we were on a first date and that Tony had picked me up. The officer told me that I could just drive the car to my home and park it in front. I was nervous, and I reluctantly said, "Okay."

I got out of the car and walked around to get into the driver's seat. I yelled to the officer to tell Tony his car would be in front of my building.

As I drove down Ventura Boulevard, I was so glad I had not had one single drink. For once, listening to my instincts paid off. Unfortunately, as I was parking Tony's car in front of my building, I suddenly realized that all I knew about Tony was his first name and home phone number. I didn't know his last name or anything else about him.

The next day I called his home number and it rang forever. I called six times throughout the day. I called again on Monday, no answer. I called again Tuesday, no answer. When I got home from work on Wednesday, Tony's car was gone and there was broken glass all around the area where his car had been parked. Tony had a Volkswagen GTI Golf with custom rims. Those cars were being stolen *a lot* in Los Angeles that year.

I called his house, no answer. I called the police to report the stolen car only to realize I had no clue what the license plate identification was. Nor did I know anything about Tony.

I went to Oil Can Harry's the following Friday and Saturday night just to find Tony.

Nothing.

I called Tony's house every day for about a month. Six weeks later I called again and the number had been disconnected. I called the phone company and told them the situation, and they said there was nothing they could do.

I never ever saw Tony again.

So what did this have to do with social media?

In 2012, even if someone only told you their first name, there are a hundred ways to find them on the Internet. As annoying as social media can be, this story gives us the lesson that it does have its benefits. However, I learned some more important lessons that night.

Never go out with someone if you only know their first name, and never let a date drink and drive.

Also, never adjust the car mirror when your date is getting arrested.

TONY
AKA: "DON'T MOVE OR
I WILL SHOOT YOU"

Adam

I liked Adam, but we had only four dates.

Date one: dinner and okay conversation.

Date two: dinner and okay conversation.

Date three: dinner and okay conversation.

Date four: we got drunk at dinner and went back to his place and got naked.

What can I say? One thing led to another. I was so swept up in the passion and nudity I was actually going to let him do *me*, which I don't normally like. One thing was leading to another, and I creatively moved my vulnerable caboose away from his train.

I asked him where he kept his condoms.

And that's when Adam said he refused to wear a condom.

"I don't like them," he said.

My thought bubble at that moment: Bridge is down and the train just derailed.

I thought to myself, *Yeah, you dumbshit, no one likes them…*

He actually said condoms are not good for you… because of the latex.

If I had a dollar for every time I had to get up and leave a date's house or apartment for something stupid said or done, I could almost buy a full tank of gasoline.

I think I know someone he could date…

**ADAM
AKA: NO GLOVE, NO LOVE**

PAUL

I met Paul at Peet's Coffee. I prefer Coffee Bean. That should have been a sign. Why do all of us constantly ignore our instincts? However, we had three fairly good dates. He was average-looking. He also seemed to have an average IQ, based on the level of our conversations.

The fourth and fifth dates were uneventful, but he hadn't pissed me off yet or said or done anything assholic. So, on the sixth date we got naked.

We were about to have sex when Paul claimed to be "allergic to condoms."

Was this seriously happening again? Another guy making excuses to not wear a condom. I must look dumb.

I said, "Really? Let's put a condom on your penis and see what happens."

Paul raised his voice, "NO, I CAN'T WEAR ONE," and he became angry.

So I said, "NO, that doesn't work for me. You see, I'm allergic to STDs and infectious diseases, and I hardly know you or where your penis has been recently."

He just looked at me, perplexed, as if I asked him the formula for glue.

If a man tells you he is allergic to condoms, make him show you the proof!

I should have given him Adam's phone number.

PAUL
AKA: CONDOM CONFESSIONS

.∎ PETER

I met Peter online. Through a Craigslist dating ad. I was pretty excited; he sounded quite hot in his description, and his picture looked good. He was not out of my league, and I was sure he would not be disappointed in meeting me either.

His description read like a pamphlet for a perfect partner who just happened to also have an amazing body.

I have a great home. I have a great job. I am good-looking and I am looking for my other half.

Wow, Peter sounded perfect for me.

Then I met Peter in person. We met at Coffee Bean near my house (no, Coffee Bean is not paying me to keep using their name).

He looked at me and said, "Wow, you are really cute."

At first I didn't believe it was really him.

Mr. Perfect looked like Mr. Perfect Liar.

He posted he was five foot eleven.

He was five foot eight. In boots.

He posted he had dark hair.

He had three dark hairs combed over the top of his bald head.

He had lied about all of his physical traits, except the fact that he was male (I think).

The photo he had posted in the ad looked *nothing* like him! Whoever Photoshopped that picture clearly had computer skills far beyond any graphic artists I have ever come across.

I am not shallow, and I didn't judge Peter only on his looks. However, someone who went that far out of their way to alter his photo is not trustworthy, or just simply too insecure.

A photoshopped picture of yourself that you are using to catch a mate is the same thing as lying.

I would have rather he pulled the normal online trick—post a picture of yourself ten years younger.

Plus, I didn't want to stick around and find out what else he had lied about, or Photoshopped, in his pants.

I looked him square in the face and said, "I don't mean to be rude, but I just don't feel anything."

I shook his hand and I got up and left.

**PETER
AKA: PHOTOSHOPPED**

▪◼ STEVEN

I responded to a dating advertisement Steven ran in an issue of *LA Weekly*. He was single and looking. It was the second, and last, advertisement I have ever replied to.

Steven should be a writer. A fiction writer.

He described himself as funny, smart, sexy, good-looking, and everything else people who create fake identities would write about themselves. What sold me, though, was that he said he had six-pack abs and worked out five days a week. More importantly, he wrote he loved his family and had a dog.

I had visions of a warrior with his chiseled body standing at the front of the battle line. Wind whipping through his hair. Post-battle, he comes charging to get me. Then, my warrior would pick me up and carry me into the sunset.

That image would soon be squashed.

I have a flat stomach and I work out a lot, but Steven's advertisement for love made me feel a little insecure. I was worried I couldn't compete with this guy, or that I was probably way out of my realm.

Still, I couldn't resist sending him a message. He replied, and we agreed to meet at a little coffee shop on Ventura Boulevard near Laurel Canyon at 7:00 p.m. He said he would be wearing a blue shirt.

I did not have a picture of him.

Again, meeting guys through ads isn't normally my style. But it was a Thursday night, so I figured I had nothing to lose. If I didn't like him, I told myself, it wouldn't interfere with my weekend schedule (even though I had nothing else to do that entire weekend).

I arrived on time. But instead of entering the shop, I peered through the window, hoping to catch a sneak peak at my future love.

What I saw instead was a middle-aged, balding,

unattractive man in a super-gay, super-tight, shiny lycra bicycle shirt. His shirt was so tight it showed off the eight-month-old baby in his belly. If he really had a six-pack, it must have been at home in his refrigerator.

I was pissed off. How dare he lie to me.

So I did what anyone who can think on their toes and has common sense would do.

I immediately walked back to my car.

I called six-pack abs from my car and told him I couldn't make it and that I was really sorry.

Then, I called my best friend, Matthew, and told him everything. Then I got a frozen yogurt, went home, and watched reruns of *Friends* on TV. Those reruns are so reliable.

**STEVEN
AKA: SIX-PACK ABS**

▪■ ERIC

Eric and I met at a roller skating rink.
Yes, people still roller skate.

Okay, I agree, it was a strange place to meet, but what the hell?

The music was on. The smell of wood varnish permeated everything. Antiquated human-size video games in the background. Red Vines at the snack counter. A shelving unit of rentable skates in the far corner. Carpeted walls a-plenty. Striped-shirt floor guards paced the joint just hoping to blow their whistles at some rebel breaking the rules.

I noticed Eric as he awkwardly skated by.

He a beginner. Me the star of the show doing tricks, jumps, and spins.

He skated up to me: "Wow, you are really good."

We chatted for a while. He was really nice and cute. I liked him. At least, I liked what I knew at that point.

When we met, he was wearing normal blue jeans, a white T-shirt, and roller blades. He looked great.

He looked masculine.

We skated around for most of the night and talked a lot. We exchanged numbers at the end of the night. We spoke the next day and made plans to go out Friday night.

He showed up right on time.

If only he had shown up on our first date in the exact same outfit he wore at the rink.

When I heard my doorbell ring, I checked myself in the mirror, checked my nostrils for boogers, then strode up to the door with a huge smile, excited for what the night would bring.

I opened the door to the past…

Eric's past.

There he was, standing in my doorway in white cowboy boots and tight white jeans. The jeans were so tight they gave him a "mammal toe" (a male vagina). And, to top off the outfit, he was wearing a white, long-sleeve, super-tight lace-up-the-middle blouse. He looked like he robbed a seriously gay pirate or a 1980s porn star.

This outfit would have been acceptable on just a few occasions:

If I were blind.

If it were 1977.

If I had no common sense.

Unfortunately, I had full vision, it was 2006, and we were in Los Angeles.

I don't know about you, but I feel what someone wears says a lot about who they are. And this man was nonverbally telling me he was a gay pirate.

We went to dinner in the most discreet place I could think of. I was actually embarrassed to be out in public with this guy. I felt like I was out with my pirate pimp aboard an extremely gay cruise. I was waiting for his gay parrot to land on his shoulder and say, "Hey girl, work it girl, you look fierce."

There would be no pirate's booty for Eric to steal that night. We arrived back at my place and I said a quick good-bye to him before his car even came to a complete stop. We never spoke again.

**ERIC
AKA: THE GAY
PIRATE, ARRGG!**

MIKE

I met Mike at the gym. Well, not the gym so much as the gym parking lot. I had seen him working out and we exchanged a nod hello in each other's direction.

It might seem like I get a lot of gym action, but given the number of times I go to the gym versus the times I have met someone, statistically, the math sucks.

Mike was very attractive, so I was happy for the unexpected connection. We talked in the parking lot for a bit and exchanged phone numbers.

We talked on the phone the following day and planned to go to a movie on Saturday. Saturday arrived, his car pulled up outside my place on time. He called and I came out.

I hate when people are late, so he scored a few points.

Then he lost them all.

As I got into his car, I realized he was on his cell phone. He didn't end the call or say anything. He just waved hello to me like he was the grand marshal in a parade and I was in the bleachers.

I had no idea what to do. Was I supposed to wave back or simply ask for his autograph?

As we started driving, I gathered he was talking to his friend about their plans for later that night, after our date. How rude. I would have forgiven a business phone call or an emergency, but this was ridiculous.

He talked on his damn cell phone the entire way to the movie theater.

My mind was racing with anger. *Am I on another planet? Is this normal first date behavior? Should I pick up my phone and make calls? Should I start texting people so I look busy too?*

By the time we got to the movie, I was going

along with what was happening against my own best judgment because I wanted to see the movie. Also, he drove, and there would be no more *walking home* dates for me.

When we got to the theater I was too annoyed to even speak to him.

I am sure in his mind I was silent and boring. That is okay.

When the movie ended, the first thing he did was turn on his damn cell phone again to check his messages. He was really annoying the shit out of me.

I know, it sounds like he wasn't that into me and I should have just gotten the clue. But through the entire movie he held my hand, and at one point he had whispered into my ear, "I love how soft your skin is, and you are so cute." He clearly was trying to turn me on—like his phone.

Aside from his sweet nothings into my ear during the movie, the cell phone thing was like being on a date with a twelve-year-old girl, calling all her girlfriends from her pink, bejeweled cell phone. I thought he was going to get off the phone to tell me how obsessed he was with *Sailor Moon* or *Hello Kitty*.

Eventually, though, I thought of a way to get even. I had to show him what he was like.

In the car on the way home, I got on my cell phone and called a friend, ignoring Mike the whole way.

He got the point.

He dropped me off at my place, and I just got out of the car and waved bye. We never spoke again.

In wasn't until later that night that the perfect solution to the whole thing hit me. I guess I should have called his cell phone from my cell phone when we were in the car. No one, I repeat, no one is so damn busy they have to be on their cell phone during a date.

MIKE
AKA: REALLY FUCKING ANNOYING

TONY

I met Tony while I was walking around a drug store looking for face soap. Why is face soap so difficult to find in stores? Is clean skin a secret?

Tony had been checking me out, and I was checking him out, and he walked up to me. Bold. Brave. I liked him already. He was handsome and manly. When we talked he seemed like a really sane guy and he gave me his phone number.

I called Tony later that night. Forget the waiting rules; I figured since he had the balls to just walk up to me and start a conversation, he deserved a call that night. He earned my attention.

We spoke for only a few minutes and then never again.

And here are the reasons why.

An hour into our call, I found out that Tony had been divorced and had a kid somewhere in West Covina that he was paying child support for. Tony was also currently married to a woman to keep her in the country, for which she paid him fifteen thousand dollars so that he could take that money and pay child support to his first wife. Tony's *current* wife didn't live with him, but was keeping all her stuff in his house in case the INS showed up.

Confused? So was I.

I got this information and much more in one phone conversation.

No first date for this tragic mess. It was a phone date, phone breakup for a relationship that never existed.

I didn't know whether to hang up, call the police, or call the FBI.

He asked me if he was telling me too much.

So I took the high road and told him that none of

what he had to say bothered me. I got off the phone as quickly as I could, and then I deleted him from my phone. It's so easy to delete people from your cell, and sometimes it feels so awesome.

In retrospect, Tony must have also been really naïve. How could he trust a total stranger with all that information? He had told me things only a mother could understand and forgive. Even that may be a stretch.

TONY
AKA: A DATE FOR THE FBI

sam

My first date with Sam actually went okay. Until the end.

In fact, I probably would have given him a second chance, except...we had the strangest good-bye.

I had picked him up and driven on the date. The date itself is not really worth discussing. I don't want to waste your precious time.

At the end of the evening I went to drop him off, pulling over in front of his apartment building.

He would not get out of my car.

I kept saying things like "I have to get up early" and "What are you up to later this week?" He let long, awkward silences lapse without saying anything.

Clearly, nothing I said was getting Sam out of my car.

He just sat in my passenger seat as the minutes ticked by. Finally, after one of the extraordinary silences went for ten full minutes, I had to say, "Okay, get out of my car so I can go!"

I'm fairly sure Sam had PADD (Potential Attention Deficit Disorder)—this is my own personal diagnosis of people I think have ADD but might never be tested.

Finally, he got out.

I never called him again, which is the easiest way to ignore someone. It was just too freaky an experience, and I don't like a lot of labor in my relationships. Trying to figure out someone else's bizarre ticks or idiosyncrasies is not my forte.

True, it is said that something worth having isn't easy to get. That sounds like crap someone posts on a refrigerator. I say that someone worth having will get the fuck out of my car like a normal person and understand the social cues that the date is over.

Plus, I don't live my life by the discourse of refrigerator magnets or coffee shop chalkboards. Bottom line, I just was not into this guy, and clearly the lights were on but no one was home.

SAM
AKA: THE CAR SQUATTER

▪◼ PILLOWCASE

Pillowcase and I met through one of my co-workers, when I was working on a very well-known television series. One of the show's producers constantly hounded me that she knew the perfect guy for me who kept asking about me. The main concern she had was that he was a cast member, and famous, so I would have to keep our date a secret. I lied and told her I am great at keeping secrets. I am not.

A secret affair with a famous actor.

This is the type of shit that goes in books.

I told her to go ahead and give him my number.

Pillowcase called, and it was a fairly decent conversation. He owned a big house in the Hollywood

Hills. He was forty-one, and I was thirty-three, which seemed like a good age difference. I like guys who are stable. That narrows the field drastically.

Our first date was at a restaurant in the San Fernando Valley on Ventura Boulevard. We had dinner and a few drinks. We then went back to his place, since my car was there.

When we got back, he invited me in for a bit. He put on some music and was clearly trying to set a mood. I appreciated his attempts. And he was really attractive. He was six foot one and had a very, very nice body. Besides, he was famous, so it was rather fascinating.

I don't normally have sex on a first date, but by that point it no longer felt like a first date. His sexual energy was putting out the vibe that he wanted to have sex. Plus, I figured I had so many other rules when it came to dating that I better let some of my rules go. I assumed it would be better to have sex on our first date and be sure we were sexually compatible than date for months only to determine that we had no sexual chemistry. I was doing a damn good job of convincing myself of a valid reason to get naked.

Still, I wasn't sure. My co-worker set us up, and if it didn't work out, it could be really awkward at work. I did not want to screw with my work environment. Also, what if the two of them were extremely close and he told her everything? What if he didn't like me? How embarrassing that would have been.

In the middle of being rational and overanalyzing the situation, I somehow wound up naked.

At first we were on his couch, and that quickly moved to his bedroom. That seems to be how most date sex progresses. We were rolling around on his bed and kissing. I was thinking to myself how smart I was to ditch my first-date rule of no sex for the night.

That is when he asked me to sit up.

He reached behind me and grabbed a pillow.

I thought he was going to toss it onto the floor or something. Instead, he quickly pulled the pillowcase off the pillow, and as serious as he could be, he said, "Tie the pillowcase around my neck really tight."

Then he mentioned something that I just can't bring myself to ever say out loud.

I was speechless. Could this be a joke? Nothing he said all night was funny. Could this be his first jab at stand-up comedy?

Nope.

Clearly he was serious.

I leapt up, got dressed, and got the hell out of there.

The following Monday morning my co-worker asked how the date went. I told her, "Trust me, I won't ever use his real name, but someday I will write about it and you will be the only person on this planet who knows exactly who I'm writing about." This is one secret I will take to the grave.

KNOWN ONLY AS: PILLOWCASE

▪■ Juan

Somehow with Juan I missed a few caution signs right from the start. Juan didn't speak English at all. And we met at a 7-11 convenience store. I was buying a cherry Slurpee and Cheetos so I could feel like a kid again. Sometimes I buy junk food to feel young and, ironically, after eating it, I feel like crap. As I left the store, he was looking at me and I was looking at him. I should have known better. But damn, he was hot and sexy as hell.

Communication was difficult because I don't speak Spanish. Growing up in Los Angeles and not speaking Spanish is a *huge* mistake, and we can blame the public school system for that. Still, we were able to communicate enough to decide that he would come over to my place the following night and would walk to dinner. Walking anywhere in LA feels like a cheap and boring version of a walk in New York. My heart and soul belong in New York. My wallet keeps me in Los Angeles.

When he got to my place for our date, the first thing he did was start ripping off my clothes. *Okay*, I thought, *I guess this is just going to be sex*. And, since it had been many months since another human touched me, I was more than ready for his offerings.

We didn't actually have sex, though. We just made out a lot.

Our clothes were off and I could not have sex with him.

No, not because I suddenly remembered my first-date rule of no sex. I simply couldn't stay erect.

His penis had a horrible, horrible odor that permeated my entire bedroom.

His penis smelled like dirty socks and cheddar cheese. I know, how disgusting, but I promised to tell you everything. When his pants dropped to the floor (commando, no undies), the room filled with the horrible scent of his uncut penis. I had never encountered that smell before in my life and it made me want to barf.

Like a middle-aged woman with too much Botox, all expression left my face.

I did not know what to do. This was an entirely new experience that caught me off guard.

I casually told him I was really tired and I needed to get to sleep. But I think he knew exactly why I got so tired.

He got dressed. I got dressed. I walked him to my front door, and he left.

I went and took a shower, even though I had just taken one an hour before. I then opened all my bedroom windows.

Poor Juan. Even though we could not communicate well, I would have been willing to work on and perhaps even learn Spanish for him. But a stinky penis is unforgivable, and the person attached to that penis is un-datable.

JUAN
AKA: DIRTY SOCKS AND CHEDDAR CHEESE

SOME GUY IN VENICE BEACH, CA

I t was late at night at a little laid-back bar in Venice that housed a pool table, video games, and a dart board. It is a cool hangout. The bar was about to close, and the 2:00 a.m. "sidewalk sale" was about to open.

He was sitting at the bar. I was with a friend, standing across from him at the other side of the bar. Now, one of the drawbacks of going to bars with a friend (same-sex at gay bars, and opposite-sex at straight bars) is that people assume the friend could be your lover. This guy, though, either didn't think that or didn't care. He and I were making eye contact and flirting like crazy.

I was imagining the two of us exchanging numbers and going to a great restaurant for our first date, where I would look great, say witty things, and we would laugh all night. That would not happen.

Then I saw him motion, à la basic sign language scrolling his hand, to the bartender for a pen, and he spoke to the bartender.

A drink was sent over to me with a note.

The napkin was folded up tightly several times, like it contained a state secret. I thought, *Gee, did this guy crack the DaVinci code and now is sharing the secret with me? Is it clues to a buried treasure?* Seriously, though, I thought, *How cute is this guy to send me a note? Is it going to be his phone number? Is the note going to tell me I'm hot? Is the note just going to say hello and have his name written in adorable handwriting because he's too shy to introduce himself?*

The passing of the note was so unique, clever, and exciting…until I got the napkin, unfolded it, and read the note:

$500 to see you naked.

I was at a loss for words—a seriously rare moment for my Energizer Bunny mouth.

My shirt didn't have the letter *A* or the word *whore* on it. Nor was I wearing clear-heeled, four-inch pumps. Nor had I just jumped down from a stripper pole.

I took my time, thinking of how to reply. I wanted to craft my response carefully.

I took the note, motioned to the bartender for a pen and wrote two more zeroes after the $500, making it $50,000. I folded it up and had the bartender hand it back to the guy.

The guy unfolded the note, read the note, looked over at me and smiled, and began to laugh. I didn't smile back. I was serious. I wanted the $50,000.

He put the note in his pocket, which further creeped me out.

I ignored him and continued my conversation with my friend at the bar.

True, this doesn't qualify as a date. But it's another story of how many fucking strange people there are in the world, and you know he would have been a horrible date. Either way, he was destined to make a page.

However, before I make myself out to be some moral hero, let's be honest. Had he stepped up to the plate and offered me the money I wanted, I assure you I'm no fool. In fact, in retrospect, I probably should have just done it for the $500.

The bar was called the Rooster Fish. I wonder if that's a code name for something I am unaware of… like Hot Dog?

SOME GUY IN VENICE BEACH
AKA: $500 TO SEE ME NAKED

NeIL

I met Neil on a chilly Thursday night at a newspaper stand in Culver City. We were both bundled up in coats. He looked adorable. I looked like a fat snowman.

I love thumbing through a good magazine, and I hope they never go out of physical print. We were both looking in the fitness section. He started talking to me. I wasn't sure if he was flirting or asking general questions, but someone told me that men only talk to people they are interested in. I don't know if that's totally true, but on some level it might be, and it was definitely true for Neil.

He asked for my number, and we spoke on the phone the following day. He lived alone in an apartment in Culver City, worked in accounting, and he was nice and really funny. I think funny people gravitate toward me because of my own fucked-up sense of humor. So when he asked me on a date, I said yes with the confidence that we had common traits.

I drove to his place. He took me to dinner at a delicious little hole-in-the-wall Thai restaurant in Culver City. I love Thai food. I love *all* food. I should be fat. Oh wait, I am on my way.

The conversation was going fine. As usual, I was starting to get excited about the possibility of a nice guy with future dating potential. And then he told me, on our first date, that he didn't want to be in a relationship but he would like to have sex with me.

How gracious of him.

Can I ask you then, Neil, why the fuck you are going on a date?

If Neil just wanted sex, he should have worn a T-shirt or sticker that said so. He was the one who asked me out on a date. Isn't the point of going on a date to see if it might turn into more dates, or a relationship? If you just want sex, there are plenty of other ways instead of dragging my ass out on a date.

I was so pissed off, I just wanted to scream out loud right there in the restaurant! I wish I would have. I would have much rather been at home eating brown sugar cinnamon Pop-Tarts.

I thought, *I took a shower and got dressed for this bullshit?*

Again, I remained civil, knowing that I was out on yet another horrible date. I got through dinner and then said good night, but I was really pissed off.

And, no, Neil did not get laid that night. At least not by me.

NEIL
AKA: WANTS TO BE SINGLE

:■ Norman

For our first date Norman and I decided to go to a movie. I realize that going to a movie inhibits conversation, but I figured we would also go grab a bite to eat or a drink afterward and would get the chance to talk then. Where and how we met is dull. We met through my friend while we were all at a bar one night. We talked on the phone once before our date.

We went to see *Babe: Pig in the City*. It was replaying in a small theater in Westwood. *Babe*, by the way, is one of the best movies I have ever seen, and I see a lot of movies. We arrived at the theater and bought some snacks. I love popcorn during a movie.

We were able to talk during the trailers shown

for other films. Norman had a lot to say. Nothing of substance necessarily, he just kept talking.

The movie started.

Norman did not stop talking.

Norman talked through the entire movie. And not with his "movie voice," or his indoor voice. You know, the quiet, soft voice everyone with common sense is supposed to use to not disturb everyone else who also paid way too much to see a movie?

It got to the point where Norman was talking so loud I had to *shush* my own date at the movie. It is really awkward to have to shush anyone in the movie theater, and it's just plain embarrassing to have to shush your own date. As if two men on a date seeing *Babe: Pig in the City* in a movie theater wasn't awkward enough?

When Norman started getting shushed by strangers, he finally realized he needed to shut the fuck up. I myself realized that if someone doesn't have enough common sense to be quiet in a movie theater, then they don't have enough sense for me to date them.

At the end of the day, it's all about how much you have in common with someone and not how different you are. While it sounds refreshing, and possibly true, that *opposites attract*, that really only applies to sex and not longevity.

Sometimes, it's the small things people do that create big impressions of what they are really like.

You can be the hottest guy in the world, but if you can't stop gabbing in the midst of the glory that is *Babe: Pig in the City*, you've got to hit the road, babe. *"That'll do, Pig, that'll do."*

NORMAN
AKA: SHUT THE FUCK UP

HENRY

Before we get into this story, I want to make clear that I think Henry is one of the most solid names a parent can give their son. It is perhaps my favorite name for a man, and I hope to meet more people named Henry. Just not more people like *this* Henry.

We met at the gym. We were both getting dressed. At first I was a bit nervous, because I was a bit sweaty and gross, but Henry did not seem to notice, or did not care. I don't shower at the gym, because I think it is creepy. I am also a mild germophobe.

We talked for a few minutes, and then exchanged email addresses and phone numbers very discreetly. Gym pickups can be so obvious and tacky. A gym pickup in the locker room is even tackier, but remember, I was slowly eliminating all my dating rules.

We spoke on the phone a few times. Henry seemed really nice. He was a little quirky, but in a good way. We made arrangements to go on a date the following week. In between, we exchanged a few emails and learned a lot of superficial information about each other: birthplace, siblings, education, blah, blah…

One week later, and apparently with not enough previous conversation, he showed up to pick me up for our first date. He was perfectly on time (a great way to start a date). I invited him in to have a glass of wine or a martini before we took off.

As he walked past me and into my apartment, I noticed the back of his hair was shaved OFF at the neckline and several inches above his hairline. Not just shaved like a normal haircut, but shaved to the point where the back of his head was bald and smooth. His hair looked like a wig resting on top of a mannequin's head.

I gingerly asked him about his haircut to see if he would tell me he was wearing a wig, which would have ended the date right there. But even a wig would have been much better than what he said.

His hair was cut like that so that THEY could recognize him when THEY get here.

Honestly perplexed and confused, I said, "Whhhat? Who?"

Then, getting a minor sense of what he might be talking about, I gave him a serious look and said, "WHAT?"

He looked up, pointed to my ceiling, and said, "Them." He paused and then said, "People from other planets. They are out there, and one day they are coming back for the rest of us, and they will only take those of us who have been acknowledging them."

I was in shock. I was at an utter loss for words.

Apparently I was not up-to-date on my "alien hairstyles" that function like a calling card for the shuttle to outer space. I suddenly realized Henry was not dealing with a full deck of cards.

I really didn't know what to do at that point.

Scrambling, I told him that I had been sick all day and didn't want to cancel, but now I realized I was just not feeling up to going out.

He had the nerve to give *me* a strange look. That's the pot calling the kettle black. He got up from my barstool, left my place, and slammed the door behind him.

I never saw Henry at the gym again. Guess he was "chosen." Lucky bastard!

HENRY
AKA: CLOSE ENCOUNTERS

TIMMY

The beginning of the spring season always seems to strike a chord with single people. Yes, everyone loves springtime. But single people think of new prospects. The trees are green. The flowers are blooming. The smell of freshly cut grass permeates the air. The five senses are working overtime.

Hormones seem to be at full attention when the weather turns from cold to warm. People seem to be in better moods. There is also the hope of seeing attractive people wear less clothing out in public. There is the hope, for us single people, that one day we will go out and accidentally meet our future soul mates. The warm weather seems to create instant endorphins.

And as spring turns to summer, the good mood seems to escalate.

In June 2003, I was at the height of my awesome summer mood and was filled with romantic thoughts of meeting someone new.

It is said that if you go out looking for something, you won't be able to find it. But when you release your thoughts and let go of desires, they seem to come at the speed of light. Sounds like more refrigerator magnet bullshit, but in my experience this is actually often the truth. However, that summer I was determined to go out in my loincloth, clobber someone over the head, and drag him back to my cave.

I was sitting outside at a patio restaurant on a warm Sunday afternoon with my friend Brent. It was one of those perfect days in LA when the weather is so amazing it seems unreal. The temperature was eighty-eight degrees and everyone was wearing very little clothing.

Lust was in the air.

We were people-watching. A favorite pastime of ours.

The restaurant where we were ogling strangers was in Studio City on Ventura Boulevard. Studio City is filled with beautiful people, because of all the out-of-work, gorgeous actors.

Then a really beautiful guy came walking down the street. And I mean REALLY beautiful. He had perfect skin. His skin had a slight glisten. He did not need to shave, because he had no facial hair. He had perfect shiny hair. He was tall with a great upper body and small waist.

We nicknamed him Eye Candy. We nickname everyone. Some people get good nicknames and some do not.

He walked into the restaurant and was seated nearby. He looked over at our table and then over at me, several times. He looked heterosexual, so I assumed he was just looking at me and wondering, *Why the hell is this dude staring at me?*

A few minutes later a very obvious, super-queeny

gay guy joined him. His friend had a small dog in a small, vented, designer purse, which is even gay for women to carry. Nonetheless, I was pleased to fantasize that Eye Candy was most likely a team player (gay).

I began to have visions of me moving in for the kill, like a velociraptor.

Brent and I tried to determine whether they were lovers or just friends. We secretly paid attention to their every move. Would they touch? Would they kiss? Would they invite me to have a three-way? Or would they give me a direct sign, a mean-girl glance, to start minding my own business? As we spied on them, Eye Candy's companion handed a red ball to him. I wondered what that was about, but I figured they played handball or something like that and soon forgot about it.

Eye Candy was masculine, a trait that not enough gay guys seem to possess for my liking, which is unfortunate. But his friend was so feminine, I was curious what they might possibly have in common.

Our food arrived, and Brent and I ate our twelve-dollar chicken salads with the dressing on the side. I wanted a side order of Eye Candy.

I noticed that Eye Candy was looking at me again. We exchanged a few smiles but without being too obvious. We were covertly trying to unlock each other's codes and secrets. It was like the *Bourne Identity*, but for gays.

Nearly forty minutes had passed and I was all out of chicken salad. I wanted to linger longer but wasn't about to resort to picking salad out of my teeth just to have an excuse to hang around. Plus, Brent and I had exhausted our shallow LA conversation: *Wanna go out tonight? Wanna go get some frozen yogurt? Who are you dating? Did you see Lady Gaga's new video? I need new jeans*, etc. Hey, let's face it, the people in Los Angeles are beautiful, but very few people here have intellectual conversations. Don't believe me? Go sit at a coffee shop in LA and eavesdrop. It is frightening.

So I was getting ready to leave when all of a sudden Eye Candy stopped by our table and said hello. I was completely surprised. Very few people in LA say hi to strangers. I do it all the time and am often ignored in return.

I know this is sounding a bit like a rag-on-LA story, but I don't want to trick you by saying the people here are fantastic; besides, you know better.

Eye Candy asked if Brent was my boyfriend. I said, "The way I was staring at you, I'd better *hope* I'm not his boyfriend."

He laughed, and I heard wedding bells.

Eye Candy was even more attractive up close. He was over six feet tall. He had an amazing body. He was mesmerizing. I was in a trance.

Most gay guys in LA have great bodies, but too often there is nothing upstairs but insulation and cobwebs. There I go again.

He told me that his name was Timmy. The name was kind of a bother, but as the years tick by my dating standards are flying away like white pigeons at a wedding. So I pulled out my cell phone and we exchanged numbers.

A few minutes later, I received a text message from Timmy:

UR REALLY CUTE.

I texted him back:

Thx u2.

He texted me:

Wher r u from?

I replied:

born n raised in LA.

He texted me again:

Im from Japan but raised here, my dad is white.

I replied:

Cool r u datin any1?

He texted me again:

> **No, or I wud not hav talkd to 2u.**

I replied:

> **Cool, do u wanna grab cofee or dinner sumtime?**

He replied:

> **Sure, what ethnicity r u?**

I replied:

> **I am a pound puppy, Im Ital, Scott n Nat Amer.**

He replied:

> **GREAT MIX, I wud rescue u.**

During all these texts I did what anyone else would do: I shared everything with my friend. Brent also thought Timmy was *hot*, and he liked his text messages. Brent was bothered by Timmy's fourth-grade name, and so was I, but Timmy had me at hello.

Later that night I called Timmy. He didn't answer his phone. He sent me a text about twenty minutes after I called:

> **Hey Eddie got yur mssg will try 2 call u ltr**

At 11:00 p.m. I got another text message from Tim:

> **Headed 2 bed, cal u 2moro, nite**

It was 2007, and text messaging had not reached the total social infestation it has today. I was new to text messaging. For god's sake I still had a flip phone. But having a college degree in communication, I was quickly realizing this was *not* real communication.

The next day rolled around, the earth continued its orbit regardless of my situation, and guess what? I did not get a call. I did not get a text.

I thought about sending him a text, but to be honest I was so annoyed by all the texting that I wanted to see if he could actually have a real conversation. So I just waited, impatiently, for an actual phone call.

Sunday came and went, no call or text. Monday came and went, no call or text. Then Tuesday afternoon I finally got a text from Timmy.

The text had no written message. But it did have an image attached. I clicked and opened the image, thinking maybe it was something romantic, funny, or cute.

It was a picture of him nude, dressed up in a leather harness, with a red gag ball in his mouth.

At first, I was speechless. Then the practical side of me kicked in and I realized that the red ball was the one from lunch.

Then, I did what most people would not do.

I forwarded the text to my sister Lisa so we could both crack up.

Then I deleted the image, and Timmy, from my phone.

TIMMY
AKA: ALL TEXT, NO SEX

▪▪ WALT

In February 2011, I was sitting on the front steps of my house and staring up at the gorgeous blue skies of Los Angeles. The few fluffy clouds in the sky looked like animals swimming and running through a calm blue ocean. I think the weather here is so amazing it could almost make an atheist believe in God.

As I was sitting there, a guy walked by with his adorable, grunting pug on a leash. He glanced over at me and said hello.

He had eyes as blue as the sky. His head was shaved, so his eyes stood out like two iridescent blue beads. His eyes would have captivated anyone. And it wasn't just his eyes. He was lean and had a body like a runner's, with no body fat. I think most people admire other people with no body fat but are also a tad jealous. I know I am, because I could never have that body type.

He walked farther down the street and then looked back at me. Then he went a little farther and looked back at me again.

I hadn't taken my eyes off him the entire time. I wasn't sure why he was looking at me, though, and he didn't look gay.

Anecdotal Note: Straight guys now dress gay, and many gay guys dress straight. Women, STOP dressing your straight men; let them go out looking horrible and mismatched! An overly quaffed straight guy is confusing for everyone.

Anyway, one more glance and he turned around and started walking back toward me. I started to get nervous. Either he was going to call me a queer, or he was going to be a queer. I figured I had a fifty-fifty chance, so I decided to wait.

He stopped and made some small talk. "Hey, how are you?"

"Great," I replied. "I'm just sitting outside enjoying this weather. It's amazing, isn't it?"

He answered with zest: "This is why I live in Los Angeles."

"Where are you from?" I asked.

He replied: "I'm from Missouri."

I thought, *Awesome, a cute, normal guy from someplace other than Los Angeles. The best-case scenario. I just hope he doesn't tell me he wants to be a singer, actor, or dancer.*

We chatted for a few minutes. His name was Walter, but he went by Walt. He worked as a graphic designer. He asked me if I wanted to go grab an iced tea or something sometime soon. The fact that he gravitated immediately to an iced tea date felt like kismet. He also said he didn't drink, because he was in AA (Alcoholics Anonymous). This was totally fine by me as long as he realized I was the opposite of AA (A lot of Alcohol).

I spoke to Walt later that night. I called him so that we could get the first phone call out of the way without either one of us having the chance to play games.

He answered his phone. Shocker!

We spoke for about thirty minutes and had a decent talk. He had two sisters. I have two sisters. He had a gay brother. I have a gay brother. It was starting to be oddly amazing how much we had in common. Could it be that Walt was the star of my long-awaited, unrealistic Disney ending?

We decided to meet up the following Friday night. I was so excited. After a few decades of dating, can you believe I still get excited to go on a date? Well, I hope you do as well. Don't ever become bitter or jaded—no one is on this planet to suffer. We are all meant for happiness.

On Friday night I sat at Coffee Bean waiting for Walt to show up. Surprisingly, he showed up right on time. *Bonus points*. When he sat down he checked his cell phone. *Minus points*.

He went in to get a drink, and I stayed outside at the table. I looked inside to see what was taking him so long, and I saw him looking at his cell phone. More *minus points*. But I still didn't think too much of it.

He was still in the game, but needed some recovery points.

Walt came back and sat down and we started talking. A few minutes into conversation, and decent conversation at that, Walt looked at his phone again. *No points left*.

I said, "Is there a call you need to take?"

He said, "No, it's cool. I just need to make sure I check my phone, because my boss is sending me some emails."

Bonus round. Full points regained. *DING DING DING*. I thought, *How great, he is really dedicated to his job*.

Walt and I sat and talked for about an hour, and several times he looked at his phone. Even though I knew it was for work, the more he did it, the more it was starting to work my nerves. But I didn't want to say anything; after all, I respect anyone who's dedicated to work.

Then Walt said he had to use the bathroom. As he walked away, I noticed he had left his phone on the table.

His phone lit up while he was gone.

Now, here is the moment where I had two options: (1) pick up his phone and make sure he really was checking emails, or (2) just wait for him to come back, trust him, and not look at his phone. I went with my instincts, of course, and did the former.

I was horrified.

Walt wasn't checking his email at all.

The entire date, Walt had been on an iPhone app called Grinder, looking for sex with strangers.

For those of you unfamiliar with Grinder, it's a ridiculous application that shows a graph of men who want to have sex with other gay men, and how many feet they are away.

Bad news for all you hetero women and men... Grinder is coming for you also. They may name it something else, but it is coming for you.

When I first heard about the Grinder application,

months before this date, I thought it was someone playing a joke on me. I thought, *This can't be for real!*

But here I was, wasting my Friday night on a fucking douche-lord asshole who was probably getting laid in the bathroom while he was on a date with me. Can you believe the complete lack of control of this guy? I hurried up and set the phone back down and put it face-down, the way I'd found it. I should have stuck my finger up my butt and rubbed it all over his phone just to be spiteful, but I didn't have the time or opportunity. Besides, he would have probably loved that.

When Walt returned from the bathroom, I took my Blackberry out of my pocket and set it on the table. I was trying to make a nonverbal point. You see, when Walt and I had spoken on the phone, he asked me what kind of phone I had. I didn't think much of it, until that moment. I realized Walt wanted to be sure I wasn't on Grinder so that our paths wouldn't cross online. (Grinder was not yet an app for Blackberry phones.)

What a major douche.

If this guy just wanted to get laid, what was the point

of meeting me for a date? When we had spoken on the phone, I told him I don't have sex with people unless I know them really well or have been on several dates. Yes, there have been some exceptions.

So after I plunked my phone down to get his attention, I got up, put my phone in my pocket, turned around, and started walking away without saying a single word to him.

While I was walking away he yelled, "Where are you going?"

I yelled back, "Turn your phone over, you douche."

As I walked away down the street, feeling totally justified in my actions, I looked up into the cold, starry, nighttime, black sky, sans cutesy animal clouds frolicking in the ocean, and said:

"Are you fucking kidding me with this shit?"

WALT
AKA: GRINDER

▪◼ NO EPIPHANY

Over my many, many years of dating, I've heard some profound, and stupid, thoughts and statements. For instance, "people on dates are on their best behavior." "Single people seem to want to be hitched." "Married people seem to want to be single."

Either way, dating is really fucking strange. Heck, I guess people are really strange in general. Take my grandfather; he truly believed I became gay because I watched too much television.

But no matter your race, gender, religious beliefs, or sexual identity, you should have been able to laugh at what, unfortunately, has been my dating reality. And even though I told you it wouldn't, I bet you thought this would end with my being happily married. Well, it doesn't.

Of course, I have also had many amazing dates with amazing people. I have had a few significant relationships in between all this dating. In fact, I'm sure I've fallen in love once, and maybe even twice. I've had true love, and I want it again. However, at the moment I am still single and dating.

And all this dating leaves me with so many unanswered questions.

Why can dating be so awkward? Should you ask a lot of questions on a date? Is it possible to ask too many questions? Do questions such as "Do you have any brothers and sisters?" make you seem like you have no depth, or does it show general interest? Does it really matter where someone is from? Assuming they don't answer with "My mother's cunt." I know my mother has one. I just don't *ever* want to know about it, think about it, or discuss it unless I'm fifteen years old again and calling it a "poon." I can laugh as much as the next person, but not about my mom's "who-ha."

Why do some dates feel like interviews? Is it because you don't like the person asking the questions? Should I start bringing my tax returns and FICO score on a date? Should I provide a list of my favorite things and just tell my date to review the list and if he wants to, he can call me later? Should I just direct people to my Facebook page?

Why does it seem most people don't know how to dress for a first date? Perhaps someone should institute a date outfit and market it to those who need our help. That way, there would at least be no surprises like über-tight white jeans, a "mangina," and white cowboy boots on a man.

And then there is the most important question of all: *By being single are we missing the boat, or are we better off?*

I would imagine you might have been on at least one or two dates that could have made the cut for this book. I hope this has been therapeutic for you to know I share your dating grief and horror stories. Perhaps you might have had some dates that were even worse than mine? I have left out a few dates that are not suitable for the printed page. (Like the guy who asked me to pee inside him after sex. GROSS!) I know, I should not have told you that, but we are grown-ups.

I'm sure there are millions of people all over the world who feel like I do. Perhaps *Dating 101* should be taught in college or high school? If not, people at least need to understand some basic unspoken dating rules. What's the point of asking someone out on a date if you are going to act like a total asshole?

It is said that going on a date actually causes a chemical reaction. It has something to do with DNA, molecules, blood flow, and the billions of neurons traveling through our bodies at any given moment. The first date in this book is proof that a bodily reaction is possible. Scientists should create a pill that stabilizes people before a date.

It is said there is a mathematical equation to determine the likelihood of finding a soul mate, partner, lover, or spouse. To get the answer to this equation, you have to factor in age, education (if that matters, and it should), likes, dislikes, race, gender, height, weight, sexual identity, and geographical desirability. I have done the math several times, and I might end up being single longer than I expected.

So for all of you who are still single, chin up and always look your best, because someday the math will be working in your favor. In the meantime, laugh, and have a wicked sense of humor. Never settle for someone who is a mess and is not right for you.

I would also suggest avoiding anyone who pulls out a hot dog during sex, "fucks their brother," or takes you to In-N-Out Burger when their cocaine high has just set in.

acknowledgments

I want to thank everyone who bought this book and laughed. I think laughter is the most important thing in life, and we need laughter now more than ever. Remember, this book is dedicated to you, so I first and foremost thank *you*!

I would like to thank Peter Lynch at Sourcebooks for believing in me, and this book, and for having a fantastic sense of humor. I would like to thank the entire team at Sourcebooks: Dominique, Liz, Lindsey, Michelle, Holly, Jill, Kay, and Lauren Panepinto. I want to thank my entire family: my mom, my sisters, my brother, nieces, nephews, my aunts, uncles, and cousins. I am grateful for my family. My Aunt Kathy and Uncle Rick taught me the importance of family and love. My Aunt Faith Lazzari taught me beauty and kindness. I want to thank my best friend, Matthew Rosenthal from Prevent Hate, for his eternal support, love, guidance, humor, and kindness. I want to thank Greg Meng and everyone at Corday Productions. I want to thank Michelle Alicea, Brian Kent, Raffles, John Walker, and Mike Walker for being profound beyond his own comprehension. I want to thank Sabrina, Little Stacey, and Dawnne for a lifetime of friendship. I want to thank Sally Abramowitz for loving me when I needed it more than she could have known.

I want to thank James Van Praagh for being an amazing person and friend. James is a gem of a human being, and his books constantly give me growth. I want to thank Debra Wilson for being an amazing life force. I want to thank Chad Allen for his love and great heart. I want to thank my Italian grandmother, "Dada," for raising me. She is one awesome lady! She is ninety years old and still doing her thing. I also want to apologize to Dada for having to read this.

:■ ABOUT THE AUTHOR

Photo by Michelle D. Alicea

I n 2005, I was working on the television series *Ghost Whisperer*, starring Jennifer Love Hewitt. I was walking down the production offices hallway one day. As I walked past one of our executive producer's offices, he called me in and said, "Hey, Eddie. What's going on with you, what are you up to? Sit down for a minute."

I sat down and replied, "Nothing, really. I'm just plugging along working on the show."

He said, "No, what are you really up to?" He paused and stared at me. "Are you writing something?"

I hesitated, but replied, "Well, if you can keep a secret, I'm actually writing an episode of *Ghost Whisperer* that I already registered and want to submit."

He looked me dead in the eye and said, "No, that's not going to happen. Stop writing that. You are going to become an author, you're going to write books."

I was speechless. No one in the world knew I was writing anything, because I *never* told anyone.

My entire body got goose bumps. How did he know?

The producer who predicted my future is world-renowned medium, psychic, celebrity, and multiple *New York Times* bestselling author James Van Praagh.

He was right.

This is my second book.

...

Eddie Campbell was born and raised in Los Angeles. He has also lived in Phoenix and Las Vegas. He once deliberately stood in the eye of a hurricane in North Carolina just to see if it was anything like the movie *Twister*. It was not.

As a child he created his own language called *gucci mala*, which he shared only with a Mattel doll named Talking Cynthia. As a teenager, Eddie was in a car accident with his best friend Liora. He went through the windshield and walked away without a scratch. He is convinced he has nine lives, but eight of them are used up.

Eddie has an associate's degree from Santa Monica College. He has a bachelor's degree from USC Annenberg School of Communication and a degree from USC School of Cinema-Television. All of his college degrees are with cum laude honors, which he credits to his memory and not his intellect. He put himself through college by being a full-time, live-in au pair raising an autistic boy who is still a major part of his life. He believes this experience was his most profound and rewarding accomplishment so far.

Eddie's background prior to becoming an author was as an art director in the art department for film and television. Some of the projects he has worked on include *Dawson's Creek*, *The Division*, *Peaceful Warrior*, *Ghost Whisperer*, *MADtv*, *The Closer*, *Parenthood*, and *Savages*.

...

UPCOMING BOOKS

Really Fucking Annoying, a book of therapeutic release
   More Horrible Dates, other people's stories from all
over the world

...

To follow Eddie, contact him, share your worst date, and get his latest news go to:
   www.eddiecampbellonline.com.

You can also follow Eddie on Twitter:
   @44horribledates.